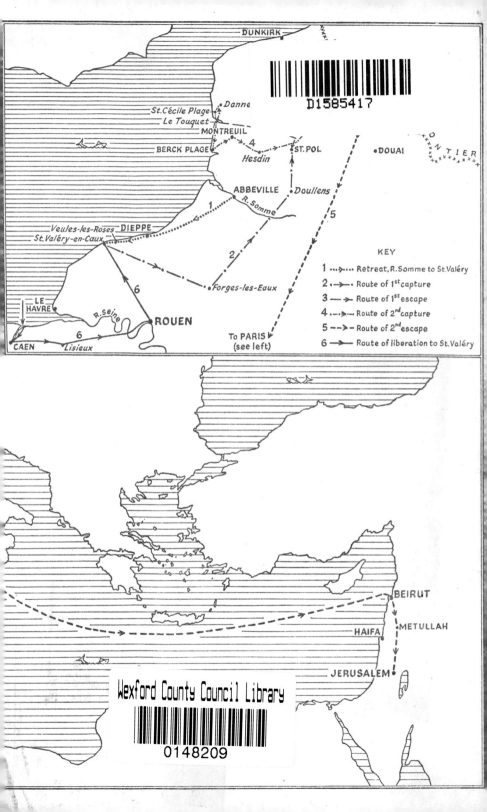

DUNKIRK

·Danne
St.Cécile Plage·
Le Touquet·
MONTREUIL
BERCK PLAGE· · · · · · · 4 · · · ·> · · ·> ·ST. POL   ·DOUAI
                        Hesdin
ABBEVILLE
                R. Somme   ·Doullens
1   5
Veules-les-Roses — DIEPPE
St.Valéry-en-Caux·· · · · · · · · · · · · · ·
                2·
                        ·Forges-les-Eaux
                6
LE
HAVRE·
        R.Seine   ·ROUEN
        6
CAEN   Lisieux   To PARIS
                                (see left)

O N T I E R

KEY

1 · · ·>· · · · Retreat, R.Somme to St.Valéry
2 ·——>—·   Route of 1ˢᵗ capture
3 ——— >   Route of 1ˢᵗ escape
4 ·——·>·   Route of 2ⁿᵈ capture
5 — — ->   Route of 2ⁿᵈ escape
6 ———>   Route of liberation to St.Valéry

·BEIRUT

HAIFA·   ·METULLAH

JERUSALEM·

RETURN TO ST VALÉRY

Return
to St Valéry

*The story of an escape through
wartime France and Syria*

DEREK LANG

LEO COOPER · LONDON

First published in Great Britain 1974 by
LEO COOPER LTD
196 Shaftesbury Avenue, London WC2H 8JL

Copyright © Derek Lang 1974

ISBN 0 85052 168 8

Printed in Great Britain at
The Garden City Press Limited
Letchworth, Hertfordshire
SG6 1JS

TO MORNA

Foreword

by ERIC LINKLATER

Stories of escape have long been popular, and as the main part of Derek Lang's story is a record of escape—from the Germans who took him prisoner at St Valéry—it is assured of welcome. It has, however, more to recommend it than the remembered thrills of a dashing retreat from intolerable confinement. It is a simple story, told with patent honesty, and though it has fewer exciting incidents than some others of its sort, it has, for compensation, an engrossing start, a charming conclusion, and a most generous appreciation of the kindliness of quite ordinary French people—of their bravery and the dangers they so willingly accepted in undertaking to help British soldiers to evade the enemy: the General has little respect for the French army and its conduct in the war, but for the uncommitted people behind it he shows, in a most warm-hearted way, his continuing affection. And that, in a soldier's narrative is gratifying; for in their remembrance of 1940 and 1941 there have been few who wrote affectionately about French townsfolk and an almost silent peasantry.

Derek Lang begins his story—most properly and justifiably—with a brief memory of the invaluable spirit of the Territorial Army which, in 1939, obediently doubled its numbers when Hore-Belisha declared that to be necessary; and a few months later, when the Highland Division moved into France to oppose on the Somme the massive advance

7

of the Germans, it revived the courageous temper of the old 51st and quickly showed a gift for war which had managed to live, through a decade that had little to recommend it, as an instinctive notion of that ultimate policy which must rely on self-defence. How well he describes the rush—from Nairn to the far-flung islands of the west—to reinforce those great regiments of Camerons, Seaforth, Gordons, Argylls and The Black Watch! Almost overnight they were doubled —nowhere in Britain was recruitment equalled by the speed of enlistment in the Outer Isles—and between the Somme and St Valéry the Camerons and the Seaforth fought with a dedicated courage.

So much for a start—which is the true foundation of Derek Lang's story—and so into the middle, which describes, with minute and loving detail, the help which he and a couple of other officers almost unfailingly got from simple French families on their precarious route to safety. This is really the wealth of the story, for the General does not conceal the fact that much of his flight was burdened by sheer boredom and constant anxiety about finding enough money to bribe people ahead of them to be persuaded into giving help.

It is an honest story, owing nothing to exaggeration of the incessant danger which attended it, but illumined—far beyond others of its sort—by its warm recollection of those who helped Derek and his occasional companions in their arduous marches to the south. There is, moreover, the supremely satisfying conclusion when the General, then commanding a Battalion of his own Regiment in the re-vived 51st Division, returns in triumph to St Valéry and meets again—with triumph and kindliness on both sides— those who had helped each other in times of dire distress. It is a most engaging tale, illumined by its affection for Scotland's old ally.

Preface

I wrote the manuscript of this book on the voyage from Egypt to Britain, via South Africa, at the end of 1942, whilst the events were still vivid in my mind. My late wife, Morna, whom I had married in Cairo in October of that year, and to whom this book is dedicated, took my dictation and bashed at her typewriter for days on end. Security forbade publication during the war and once it was over the world wanted to forget it, so there was only a limited market for escape stories. I read some that were published with great interest and a sense of humility. My manuscript was put away in a box where it has collected dust these past thirty years. Now my story is part of history.

I am much indebted to Major Douglas Sutherland, MC, author and journalist, who has painstakingly helped me re-edit the manuscript. With his help and because of the passage of time it now has a beginning and end which previously it lacked. My thanks are also due to General Frank Richardson for his encouragement, advice and research; to Mr Hugh Hanning for recommending my manuscript to Leo Cooper; to Leo Cooper for risking me; and to my long-suffering wife, Elizabeth, who has guided me over the format and, despite her Hungarian upbringing, has corrected my clumsy prose.

I am extremely grateful to that great Scottish author and historian, Eric Linklater, for his foreword. Eric Linklater has always had a particular affection and admiration for the

Highland Territorial and has aptly related my personal experiences with the tributes I wanted to pay not only to those who assisted me, but to the military "family" which enshrouds all of us soldiers individually and gives us the will and pride to survive and succeed. The Territorials—twice citizens—still thrive as they did in the thirties and forties. Sadly there are now fewer of them, but they are today more professional and better equipped.

My story was written when I was a young man, is seen through a young man's eyes and told in a young man's words. It hides none of my feelings of fear, elation and inadequacy. I believe young people now would have the same emotions, but would they make the same mistakes? My contemporaries may enjoy the opportunity for reminiscence and bore their friends and relations with their tales of "I was also there", or thereabouts. Those closely involved with me at the time can derive pleasure or anger criticising my inaccuracies, for even though most of the script was written soon after the events, I am certain to have made errors in recording them.

I hope that my book shows sufficiently how much I, and so many others, owe to the courage and determination of those civilians, particularly the women, who risked their lives protecting us. As Mr Harold Macmillan recently said, when he spoke at the launching of his last volume of memoirs—"Old men do not forget!"

September, 1973

Illustrations

The author and publishers would like to thank the following for permission to reproduce copyright illustrations: the Dundee Courier and Advertiser, no 16, Aberdeen Journals Ltd, no 17, and Cowper and Co, Perth, no 18.

"I sought for merit wherever it was to be found, it is my boast that I was the first minister who looked for it and found it in the mountains of the north. I called it forth and drew into your service a hardy and intrepid race of men, who when left by your jealousy became a prey to the artifice of your enemies, and had gone nigh to have over-turned the State in the war before the last. These men in the last war were brought to combat on your side; they served with fidelity as they fought with valour, and conquered for you in every part of the world."

LORD CHATHAM 1766

Prologue

Is it my imagination or was that autumn of 1938 particularly unclouded and brilliant? Certainly, so far as I was concerned "God was in his Heaven and all was well with the world".

One week before my twenty-fifth birthday, I was made an acting, unpaid Captain in my Regiment, the Queen's Own Cameron Highlanders, and appointed as Adjutant to our only Territorial Battalion—the 4th. As promotion went in the Regular Army in those days I was very young for the job. I took over from a man thirteen years my senior and, if I had any worries at all, it was that I should not live up to my new responsibilities.

To date in my career my responsibilities had not been over onerous. I had never had any doubts about what I was going to do in life. Neither had my father. He had been a Colonel in the Indian Army and, being very proud of his Scottish ancestry, was anxious that I should follow his career, but in a Scottish Regiment. To this end after school and Sandhurst I managed to get into the Regiment of his and my choice.

I am afraid that once I had achieved this first hurdle in my ambition, I did not take the professional aspect of my new life very seriously. Who did in those days? I played polo and shot sand grouse and duck in the Sudan and Egypt, and made excursions up both the Blue and the White Nile in pursuit of buffalo and antelope. I flirted with well-chaperoned British girls who were overseas seeing the world and spent much of my duty time in athletic competitions, playing rugby, boxing, or shooting on the army ranges with the men.

True I spent a few months in 1936 skirmishing with the Arabs in Palestine, but this did little more than add some spice to life and three of us spent most of one leave in August that year on a trip home by car via Greece, Bulgaria, Romania, Hungary, Austria, Germany, Belgium and France. Hitler was full of bombast, staging the Olympic Games whose motif was displayed everywhere as we drove through Bavaria and the Rhineland. If this journey gave me some inkling that all was not right in Europe, I soon shrugged it off and resumed my carefree existence.

Then in the autumn of 1938, just when I was starting my new job, there came the Munich crisis and things were never quite the same again. Neville Chamberlain came back from his meeting with Hitler, declaring that it was to be "peace in our time" but only the most naïve of us believed it. The signs were there for everyone to see and if anyone had any doubts that the Government had been hoodwinked, they were rapidly dispelled when, in April, 1939, Mr Hore-Belisha, the Minister of War, ordered that the Territorial Army should be doubled immediately. The country was being put on a war footing.

I had only known the Territorial Army for a few months but it had already impressed me as a very remarkable body of men and without, I hope, being too chauvinistic, my own Battalion seemed one of the most remarkable of all. Whereas other Battalions recruited their men from comparatively limited geographical areas, mine covered a territory from Nairnshire in the east to the Outer Hebrides in the west where sheep outnumbered human inhabitants. My headquarters were in the town of Inverness, but my Companies were miles apart so that they seldom saw one another and I was the main professional link between them. That was only the beginning of dispersal for each Company had two or three collecting points for training spread over many square miles of country and the men themselves often had long distances to travel to get to the collecting points.

The only other regular officer besides myself at battalion headquarters was the Quartermaster. I also had a regular Regimental Sergeant-Major at Inverness and one senior non-commissioned officer, Permanent Staff Instructor. To add to this small full-time cadre I had five other regular instructors distributed throughout the area. There was one close by in Nairn, another in the old Wolf of Badenoch's wild country at Kingussie and another in Lochaber at Fort William where the Regiment was raised. More remotely there was one at Portree on the Isle of Skye and, further afield still, a fifth at Daliburgh in South Uist who was responsible for all Cameron Territorials in the Outer Hebrides. When I paid a visit to the Outer Isles, I had to allow several days for the journey as communications were so bad.

Whenever I visited a local drill hall I never knew whether I was going to meet two or twenty Territorials. During the harvest attendances were likely to be sparse, but in the long winter months without the distractions of television and other modern diversions, I could count on a good attendance. It depended too on the availability of the officers. These were either ex-regulars, farmers and local professional men, or carefully picked sons of lairds who were living and working in the south. They were all splendid people, but even though they were enthusiastic and enjoyed their tenuous link with the Army, one seldom saw those based far afield except during the annual fortnight's collective camp.

Every summer we held this annual camp but attendance was not compulsory and there were many men who either could not or would not find the time to make the journey. Indeed, the lack of equipment made most of these affairs little more than social gatherings. Travelling expenses were paid to those attending and this brought us into constant conflict with Whitehall who seemed to imagine that the Hebrides were situated somewhere in the Moray Firth. Nor could they grasp that there were few railways and most journeys had to be made by hired car or boat. Islanders had seen aeroplanes, but not trains.

Before my time the General commanding the Highland Division in Perth toured our more remote territory. He was an Englishman and, I fear, he fared badly for the sturdy islanders had little respect for the "top brass". I felt, however, that he began to realize some of our difficulties when he had to take the old ferry route from South Uist to Benbecula, which meant either a boat or horse and cart, dependent on the tide. There was no bridge as there is today. When the ferryman was asked if he had received a signal about the visit so painstakingly planned in Perth (all messages were then delivered by hand) and whether there was a car to meet the General at the other side, he replied that he recollected getting a note, but thinking it to be of "no importance", had thrown it into the sea! The General had to continue his journey, first by boat, and then by horse and cart.

What is important to the Outer Hebridean, particularly the people of South Uist, is piping. Who will contradict me if I say that the finest bagpipe players in the world come from South Uist? Is it the loneliness, the solitude, or the atmosphere? Whatever it is, in those pre-war years, the locals beat all comers in competitions, and the best of Scotland and further afield came to compete at their simple annual games held on the Machar or Links, just north of Lochboisdale.

The enthusiasm of our men varied considerably, but I often felt that my visits to talk to them were too often treated as a form of light entertainment. We had a fair contingent on Skye, but we needed more. I once asked the management of the Talisker Whisky Distillery if the men could have time off in the morning so that I could address them. This was very kindly agreed and I found myself faced with a gratifyingly large audience sitting on grain sacks in a large half-circle. I was making an impassioned and, I thought, rather effective plea for more recruits when the lunch-time hooter went. Without a word they rose to their feet to a man and filed out leaving me in mid-sentence. No recruits that day!

It can readily be realized that when the order came to double our strength overnight from a rather uncertain five hundred to twelve hundred I viewed my task with some misgiving. I had reckoned, however, without two factors which were to work to my advantage. One was the intense patriotism of the Scottish Highlanders and the other was the great influence over tenants exercised by the lairds, many of whom, or their sons, were officers in my Battalion.

The Highlands have been one of the most fertile recruiting grounds for the British Army since Bonnie Prince Charlie's ill-fated rising. I was operating in the Young Pretender's country where family and clan loyalties had not changed all that much since 1745. The problems facing me were somewhat more complex than they had been two hundred years before, but the spirit was still the same. Macdonalds were prominent Prince Charles Edward supporters and so they were now for the 4th Camerons. In one Company we had thirty-five Macdonalds. Individual recognition was further complicated by the fact that ten of them

17

had the name John. Despite the fact that Christian names were used freely we had to resort to military numbers to differentiate one from another in this instance.

By no means the least of the advantages I had was in the person of Evan Baillie, of Dochfour, who was our Colonel. He was a man of boundless energy and influence and he threw himself into the campaign for recruits with the utmost enthusiasm.

I was in Lochmaddy in North Uist when I first received news of Hore-Belisha's call to arms and, there being no telephones on the islands in those days, I telegraphed to Evan Baillie for instructions. If I had expected a curt military reply I could not have been more mistaken. Nor could the postmistress at Bayhead Post Office in the west of the island to which his reply was directed two hours later. The only two telegraph forms available were soon exhausted; the backs of envelopes were called into service, and, finally, in desperation, a toilet roll was requisitioned as the message ran on and on. I was to find new recruiting centres on the islands, open up territories like Harris which had been untouched for years and, in short, raise a "fiery cross" from end to end of the Hebrides.

Our Islands Company Commander, Viscount "Dubby" Fincastle, whose family had long territorial associations with Harris, came to join me and the local Permanent Staff Instructor, whose name, not surprisingly, was Macdonald. We set up our base at Leverburgh, the site of the late Lord Leverhulme's ill-fated attempt to improve the economy of the island, and soon Dubby's men started to roll in. It was not everywhere, however, that we met with such success. When we landed on the little island of Berneray, the fisherman population hid from us either among the rocks or behind their locked croft doors, no doubt remembering tales of the old press gangs.

In South Uist I received the greatest help from a formidable figure, Finlay Mackenzie, who treated me like his own son when I was in his domain. Finlay was the proprietor of the Lochboisdale Hotel and many regarded him as the real laird of the area. Finlay had led an extraordinary career which included service with the Canadian Mounties and he had been a 4th Cameron in the twenties. The great of those days came frequently and felt privileged to stay with Finlay to catch fish, shoot snipe and enjoy his hospitality. Woe betide them if they could not drink dram for dram with him. Many who couldn't were not welcomed back. He put his two old Rolls-Royces (the only cars on South Uist) at my service and himself stumped from end to end of the island, exhorting and cajoling the crofters into joining. The great-hearted Finlay was in his sixties but his dearest ambition was to lead his own men into battle. When this was refused him because of his years, he was inconsolable.

This pattern of exhortation and natural patriotism proved effective all over our area. I believe that the London Scottish were the first to reach their target figure but the Camerons were not far behind. In June, 1939, we mustered in camp near Dundee, sixty officers and twelve hundred men strong. They came in every form of dress and from every walk of life. They were not only crofters and fishermen, but bank clerks, lawyers and accountants, and even two forty-year-old stockbrokers from London.

I well remember our first church parade when we were to show ourselves off before the British Legionaires at an open air drumhead service. I had been told to find a choir and in time-honoured fashion had deputed the task to the Regimental Sergeant-Major. When the great day came I found that there was no choir and asked the R.S.M. what had happened. "Quite forgot it, Sir," he confessed, "but don't worry." Marching down the front rank of assembled men, he laid his staff on the shoulder of the twelfth man and shouted, "Here to the right, right turn—Choir!" We were back in business.

When war was finally declared in September our dispersed forces were mobilized in Inverness. Picture what was involved collecting over a thousand men together from the vast expanses of Inverness-shire and Nairnshire by sea and road. There were no ships or lorries that could be requisitioned and we had to rely on the infrequent public transport services. I had the temerity to demand naval escorts from the Admiralty to protect our contingents crossing the Minch and got the outraged refusal I deserved. However, the redoubtable Finlay rose to the occasion again and in the absence of our own officers, who could not get to the outer isles in time, brought the Uist boys across safely like a hen with her chicks. The sight of him marching in at the head of his own men, wearing his civilian kilt in a last vain hope of being able to join us, will ever be remembered by those of us who saw it.

To our dismay Evan Baillie was passed unfit for active service and his command was taken by Earl Cawdor, third in command a few months earlier; the second in command, Alec Cattanach, now being faced with the task of organizing from scratch the 5th Camerons, formed as a result of doubling the 4th. Alec's right-hand man as Adjutant was Jock Maitland Makgill Crichton, who had come to my rescue as Assistant on the order to double the T.A.

Tradition distant and recent was maintained. Lochiel's Camerons from Lochaber had rallied to Prince Charlie in the '45 and the 25th Lochiel had raised and commanded the 5th Camerons in the 1914–18 war. Now his youngest son, barely out of school, joined this newly formed 5th Battalion, which again included the men of Lochaber.

20

With only rifles and old Lewis guns our home-spun army, full of *esprit de corps* but sadly lacking in military training, was sent down to Aldershot in October where we spent most of our time drawing vehicles and other equipment and trying to fit all the pieces together. Three months later we were on active service in France and by the early spring of 1940 in contact with the Germans, the most highly trained army in the world, in the Saar.

I suppose we were at least fortunate that we had had the period of the "phoney war". During the past three months we had become adept in the art of moving as a military body if little else and discipline was improving all the time. In April we were directly in front of the famed Maginot Line. We found ourselves manning our sector of the front from ill-prepared defences like grouse butts. There were many things to admire about the French Army, but their preparation of proper defences in the front and rear of the Ligne Maginot was not one of them and time and time again we found ourselves faced with the task of extensive digging when taking over a position from them. Too much faith was put in the concrete-built Maginot itself and the three lines fore and aft, to give it depth, were ignored.

Our first night in the "grouse butts" proved most unfortunate. The Germans who, being locally recruited, knew every inch of the ground, observed our arrival with interest and glee. The unit which we relieved reported to us that all had been quiet but our opponents obviously thought it would be profitable to make an unexpected raid on the newcomers. They opened up with a spectacular show of fireworks using tracer ammunition and grenades. In the light of later experience it was only a minor affair, but it shook us up considerably. A number of men behind our scant defences were shelled, raided and captured. For us all the war had suddenly started in earnest.

It was shortly after we had been relieved of our front line position that the invasion of Belgium took place. This resulted in our being rapidly transferred to the northern sector, it being realised that the Germans intended to by-pass the much vaunted Maginot Line. We travelled by train and the whole operation was tragically chaotic. The train was so old that on one occasion we all had to climb out to push it up a hill. I still laugh when I think of it. Eventually we arrived in the region of Rouen having taken a long circular route south of Paris in the rear of what was still left on the Continent after Dunkirk of the British Expeditionary Force.

We had no sooner made camp than we began to hear the most horrific rumours about the German advance. Rumours in the rear echelons are usually exaggerated but it soon became obvious that the position was indeed serious.

The Highland Division were now the only remaining organized British Infantry formation in France and we were ordered to take up a position to the left of the French. By the beginning of June we were on the Somme, of such bitter memories in the Great War, and the stage was set for one of the greatest catastrophes in our military history.

Our morale was at first raised by the news that the German bridgehead opposite Abbeville had a day or so before been magnificently reduced in size by a gallant French attack, under the young General Charles de Gaulle. We now came under his command and our task, supported by French tanks, was to drive the enemy back completely across the river. Battle however is not that easy—the enemy had been strongly reinforced in the interim.

Jack Cawdor and Colin Hunter, our intelligence officer, attended de Gaulle's orders for the Divisional attack and only the other day Colin described to me the feeling he had on that occasion that he was in the presence of a very great man.

The fourth of June will long be remembered by the Highland Division as the day when we went into the attack. Abler pens than mine have described this desperate battle and this book is not an account of a campaign. Suffice to say that by nightfall we could only muster a total of three hundred and fifty officers and men from a total strength of six hundred who had advanced with such confidence a few hours earlier. Regimental Headquarters sited in a beautiful chateau in the village of Hurchenneville was surrounded by mutilated bodies lying all over the garden waiting to be evacuated by the overworked ambulances and we knew the bitterness of a crushing defeat.

The memory of the first onslaught of war always lives vividly and longest. I lost three of my closest friends in those few hours on the Somme—all Company Commanders —two killed and one taken prisoner. The eight days of retreat culminating in capture at St Valéry-en-Caux, starts my escapades. I hope this first chapter prologue gives not only a worm's eye view of the gallantry and dedication of our Highland Territorials who were amongst the first of our citizen forces to see action in the Second World War, but also shows the impossible conditions under which they were asked to fight. This book, apart from being my personal story, also tells how the 4th Camerons in 1940, were revenged by their 5th Cameron brothers in 1944, and how staunch and patient were the French in the intervening years. Charles de Gaulle made the now famous statement— "The valiant 51st Highland Division played its part in my decision to continue fighting on the side of the Allies."

Chapter 1

Some of the finest and bravest actions fought by the British Army, like Fontenoy and Corunna, have been when they have been in retreat. I am not saying that the eight days which were now to follow were by any means Britain's finest hour but I was to find out at first hand something about the indomitable spirit of the British soldier in adversity.

The order to retreat came on 5 June. After the drubbing we had received morale was not high but we still wanted to stand and fight. Yet from the overall tactical point of view retreat was inevitable. The French were falling back on both flanks and we could not afford to run the risk of having our whole force cut off. What everybody dreaded most was to be captured and spend the rest of the war behind wire. I think we all knew somebody who had been a prisoner during the Great War and it was an experience we did not want to try.

During the first day of the retreat we covered about eight miles over country which was as flat as a pancake. The sun blazed down and there was no water to be had. It was a terrible sight to see the men, exhausted from their recent battle, strung out in straggling lines like a lot of refugees. It was impossible to keep them in any sort of military formation. It was a case of doggedly plodding on in the footsteps of the man in front. With three other officers I brought up the rear. Every now and again we had to pull men up from where they had fallen, fainting from the heat or simply at the end of their tethers from fatigue. We had to be pretty brutal, dragging them out from under the hedges and kicking them to their feet in an effort to make them carry on.

At one point I found an anti-tank rifle where it had been thrown in a bush. With some vague idea that it was disgraceful to abandon arms in the face of the enemy I picked it up and carried it for many miles until I could carry it no longer. It was in fact a fruitless waste of energy.

All through that long, excruciating day the Luftwaffe flew in circles over our heads. How we longed to see some British aircraft, but they never came. Instead the German fighters dived so low that the black swastikas on their wings were clearly visible and at times they machine-gunned our poor struggling column. Their complete command of the air added to our general feeling of wretched depression.

Occasionally we passed through villages, deserted by their inhabitants and reduced to rubble by shell-fire, the smoke still rising from their burnt-out buildings. I remember particularly in the little village of Hurchenneville, just behind our late battalion headquarters, an old lady sitting quite alone on the doorstep of her bombed cottage. As we passed she gave us a brave wave, defiant to the last and still able to wish us luck in our common adversity. I was so touched that I went over to her and begged her to let us take her with us, but she would not be moved. She had lost everything but her spirit was unbroken.

When we reached our first temporary defence position at the end of the day on a railway line near Martainneville, we had an opportunity to reorganize the Battalion. The whole of one Company had been captured and the others were so depleted that we were only able to form a Battalion Headquarters and two composite Companies, commanded by Stanley Hill and Bertie Macleay, both veterans of the

Great War whose example was an inspiration to us less experienced officers. As dawn broke we were joined by a contingent of some sixty stragglers who had somehow been collected by a young subaltern, David Ross, and extricated from the chaos. It was a splendid achievement and greatly cheered us.

Late in the afternoon of the following day we caught sight of the advance elements of the enemy. They were creeping down the tracks in some nearby woods in heavily armoured trucks. They were still some distance away when we were startled to be invaded by some French anti-tank gunners who came rushing through our lines, shouting "Les Bosches! Les Bosches!" and urging us to join them in their headlong retreat. They had completely lost their nerve and the incident did nothing to improve our own morale.

Although much has been written in criticism of the French Army during the invasion of their country in 1940, they had some splendid fighting soldiers. We had a battery of French 75's supporting us on the Somme who put up a magnificent performance. It did our hearts good to hear the brave whine of their shells whenever the Germans stopped firing.

We now hoped that we would be allowed to stay and fight but it was not to be. That night the order came to withdraw again back to Blangy through which we had passed with so much confidence a few day's earlier. We were furious at thus giving the Germans such an easy passage but as we started to move back again we met a contingent of French machine-gunners going forward to cover our withdrawal and we gave them a hearty cheer of appreciation.

There was a slight panic in the beginning because Stanley's Company, which had been a little distance detached, failed to join us at the appointed hour. Sending on the main party, some of us stayed by the roadside in the hope that they would still turn up. It was an eerie feeling, waiting in the blackness, not knowing whether it would be Stanley's Jocks or the Germans who would turn up first. Shortly after midnight we heard the tramp of approaching soldiers. To our great delight it turned out to be our men, exhausted but marching in perfect formation with gallant "Daddy" Hill at their head.

Blangy was a sad sight. The attractive little French town lay in ruins. Just after we had passed over the two bridges we heard the satisfactory sound of them being blown up. Then we found ourselves in the pitch darkness surrounded by French troops, both coloured and white, who seemed to be in the last stages of panic. All around us men shoved, jostled and shouted to get into a front place. It was a really sickening scene, particularly as we were sure that the Germans were many miles behind with the river still to cross. That night we joined our transport in the Forêt D'Eu and the men had their first opportunity of a hot meal for a week.

One of the things by which we set much store in the days which followed were the B.B.C. communiqués, although most of them concentrated on the fighting further south. It appeared that the French in their sector were retiring even more rapidly than we were. Once we were told that they were resisting strongly and that the R.A.F. were operating in force at all points of the front. As we had still not seen a single British plane we took this with a pinch of salt. In fact it became obvious to us that we were to be pushed out of France and our main anxiety now was how we would get back over the Channel and live to fight another day.

The days started to follow a pattern. We would dig in and our hopes would rise at the thought of having a crack at the enemy and then each evening there would come the message to retreat again. There were only occasional skirmishes and every now and again we would be strafed from the air but on the whole we had the uncomfortable feeling that we were running away from nothing. There is no worse feeling for a soldier but there was no alternative but to obey orders.

Then one morning we watched in awe as a force of two hundred German bombers flew over our heads. It was not long before we learned that they had succeeded in their mission to wipe out our supply depots in the Havre area. From then on we got no supplies from base and had to live off the country.

The French civilians who had remained behind were truly marvellous. Wherever we stopped a message would come from the nearest chateau telling us to take what we wanted. They were determined to prevent anything valuable falling into German hands and pressed us to take all they had including liberal supplies of wine.

It was on the fifth day of the retreat that we received the alarming message that there had been a complete breakthrough to the south-west and that the Germans were already in Rouen. At the same time we had the first firm orders since we had started. We were to make for Le Havre as fast as we could where the Royal Navy was waiting to ferry us back to England. This was great news. At least we knew where we were and what was being done for our salvation. To speed our progress all non-essential equipment, which was normally carried in transport, was made into a huge pile and burnt so that everyone could be lifted instead of marching.

With optimism we piled into the trucks and set off as fast as we could motor. It was not a mood which lasted long. We had only done about twenty miles when we learnt that the road to Le Havre was cut and that we were to make our way to the little fishing village of St Valéry-en-Caux. It is a name which will be forever remembered in the annals of the 51st Highland Division.

That night was for me a night of near despair. We were forbidden to use any lights and the darkness was impenetrable. Part of our convoy had disappeared in the blackness and I set off on the back of a motorcycle, ridden by my assistant adjutant, Roddy MacLeod, to try and locate them. It was a hopeless task, made all the less appetizing by not knowing where the enemy were and having a constant feeling that we might run slap into them round the next corner. In the end we gave up the search and returned to the main column only to discover that they too had now disappeared. A further frantic journey followed which only ended with us catching up with them as dawn was breaking and the motorcycle was on its last few ounces of petrol.

Hope was revived the next day. The enemy were nowhere in sight and we were told to take up a defensive position round St Valéry, to which we were to withdraw after dark and be evacuated. In the meantime an order was given for everyone to get rid of all their personal kit. In the carefree winter of 1939 we had listened to friends who had advised us to bring over as many of our possessions as we could to increase our comfort. Fortunately I had a tin trunk with me in which I kept my things. Rather than destroy them I told my batman to bury the trunk in a nearby orchard and make a careful note of the site. For some strange reason I hoped to be back for it!

We lay up quietly all that day blissfully ignorant that the Germans, under an as yet unknown General, Rommel, were closing in on us from the west. Occasionally we heard the crump of shells and bombs directed at the port behind us but none of us imagined for one moment that there was anything serious enough to interfere with our safe evacuation.

At midnight we gathered together what few pitiful things we had left and moved in perfect order down from our positions to the little town.

We had, of course, been out of sight of St Valéry all day so we had no idea what to expect. What we found far exceeded our worst fears. As we filed down from the hills above the town we saw that it was ablaze. Great spurts of flame were visible from some distance off and, when we reached the outskirts, we were confronted with streets jammed with every conceivable kind of vehicle. Men were rushing about in all directions so that the whole scene was hopeless chaos.

I imagined that somewhere in the holocaust there was some sort of British Higher Command trying to operate but it was immediately obvious that I should never be able to make contact with it. The only solution seemed to be to make for the beach and to try to reach the ships which were to take us off.

It was a vain dream. Along the promenade there were groups of men large and small clustered together in the light of the burning buildings, bent on the same mission as myself. As for the ships there was no sign of one to be seen. To add to my misery it started to rain in one sustained torrential downpour.

It was low tide and all the local boats were beached upstream on the mud flats so there was no escape that way. A few parties tried to make their way out onto the sandy shore. Immediately from the cliff tops there opened up a steady stream of machine-gun fire. The Germans had crept in behind us as we withdrew from our positions and now commanded the beach from the heights on the west. With the whole front ablaze we were silhouetted against the furiously burning fires and completely trapped.

Our troops got under such cover as they could while I went in search of Brigade or Divisional Headquarters, though what they could have done I did not know. At least they might have had some ideas about the general situation. As I passed amongst the great crowds—there must have been twenty thousand there that night—I heard cries of "Help the wounded to escape first", but there was none who had any ideas how this was to be accomplished. There were wounded everywhere and I could hear anguished cries from civilians inside their battered houses.

At about four in the morning, I gave up and tried to find somewhere to sleep for the remaining hours before daylight. Eventually I found one of the few houses left standing. It was packed with bodies, whether dead or alive I did not know or care. Improbably a middle-aged lady appeared from somewhere and asked me if I would like her to dry my clothes. I was soaking wet but past caring. Within minutes I was fast asleep.

When dawn finally broke and we were able to see more of what was going on around us, we were elated to pick out the shape of half a dozen warships on the horizon. We had them under observation for an hour or more and then, to our intense despair, they steamed away from shore and disappeared altogether. Whether these ships were French or English I did not know nor did I know then why they made no attempt to come to our rescue.

Hope rose again later when two ships were spotted lying close inshore three to four miles down the coast at Veules les Roses. I found Ian Barclay, our acting Brigadier (the Brigadier had been wounded some days earlier), wandering around like the rest of us and suggested to him that I should try to reach one of these ships. If they had a wire-

1 The author's picture taken from a contemporary identity card.

2 The beach at Veules les Roses where the author and Colin Hunter were captured.

So hatten sie sich den Marsch nach Berlin nicht vorgestellt

3 A photograph from a battered copy of the Nazi propaganda maga-
zine 'Signal' which shows the Highland Division prisoners-of-war
taken at Veules les Roses. Colin Hunter is in the centre right of the
picture with a bandaged eye and the author, half face, at the extreme
right.

less set working, which seemed possible, I would be able to get in touch with the Royal Navy and at least discover if there was any prospect of our being taken off. Ian agreed that it was worth a try so I set off taking one of our Sergeant Majors with me.

It was harder going than we had expected. We had to keep close in to the rocks to avoid attracting machine-gun fire from the cliff tops. As it was there were places where we could only advance by diving from cover to cover. As we progressed we came across the bodies of many of our soldiers and Frenchmen who had been caught in the cross-fire of the guns. Some lay at the water's edge, washed by the tide. Others were poised in standing or crouching positions against the rocks where they had been shot. They looked so lifelike that we approached several of them to talk to them only to find their eyes sightless and their bodies rigid in death. These dreadful corpses reminded me vividly of P. C. Wren's book *Beau Geste*, in which the dead bodies were propped up on the battlements of the Fort of Zinderneuf.

Evidently some of the troops had tried to descend the three hundred foot high cliffs on ropes. Few could have succeeded judging by the smashed bodies lying on the beach while a hundred and fifty feet above we could see the frayed ends of their broken ropes. Most appalling of all were the wounded. They were everywhere and on our approach called out to us for water or to help bind up their wounds. There was nothing we could do for them as any delay endangered the success of our mission on which the fate of so many depended.

It seemed an age before the two ships came nearer. The sun was high in the sky and it became hotter and hotter, adding to the agonies of the wounded. With the hard going and the heat, we discarded most of our clothing and were

33

completely exhausted when, after over two hours, we finally reached Veules. We found that the bigger of the two ships was French and was lying some way out from the shore, while the other, little more than a fishing boat, bravely flew the Red Ensign. We could see that the decks of both ships were already covered with men, both French and British. They had apparently come in the night before as part of a small rescue force and the British ship had run aground on the sand. Now there was no hope that it could get off until the next high tide later in the afternoon. The French ship had a little three-pounder mounted forward while the British only had a pair of ancient Lewis guns.

In addition to the men crowding the decks of the two ships, every bit of cover under the cliffside sheltered further groups waiting helplessly to see if any further craft were going to show up. Every now and again a group would break from cover and attempt to reach one or other of the boats. Some of the more enterprising had managed to get hold of small dinghies which they rowed out. This immediately attracted the attention of the enemy who started to shell them. Few escaped unscathed but one boat in particular seemed to have a charmed life. With the shells falling all round it, it struck bravely out into the channel and was soon only a speck in the distance. I have often wondered if it ever reached safety.

While we were taking in the scene and wondering what we should best do, the big guns on the cliffs near St Valéry opened up on the Frenchman. Bravely she replied with her three-pounder but the shells could scarcely have got half way to their target. It was not long before the German guns found the exact range and then we had a ringside seat at this macabre play, watching in horror as they systematically destroyed the crowded ship. It must have been hit a dozen times before the little gun was finally silenced and a few minutes later the riddled hulk slid over on its side.

Now the Germans turned their attention to the British ship, air-bursting their shells above it so that the whole beach was under a curtain of flying shrapnel which threw up thousands of pebbles, adding to the murderous effect of the fire. It was obvious that she could not last much longer so I decided to make a dash for her in the hope that I could find a wireless set before it was destroyed. As I clambered aboard, the first person I met was Colin Hunter, the Intelligence Officer from my own Battalion, who had thought of the same idea as myself. From him I quickly learnt that there was no wireless and that the boat was so hopelessly overcrowded that the Captain feared she would not be able to make the crossing even if she could be floated off. There seemed to be little point in my remaining as an Aunt Sally, so I returned to the shelter of the cliffs to discover that Ian Barclay had decided to join us himself to find out what was happening.

After some time the firing grew more desultory. It seemed that the Germans were waiting for something to happen. It was early in the afternoon when we discovered what it was. Firing now opened from the east and we could see enemy vehicles trundling along the cliff tops east of Veules. They were closing their pincer movement and now there was no way out. I was in a cave with about two hundred Frenchmen, most of whom were completely exhausted and broken in spirit. The only idea I had left was to gather what rifles and ammunition I could and take a party of volunteers out to the British ship to make a final stand. To my disgust I could only muster about half a dozen to come with me but set out none the less and, once aboard, we spread ourselves out in between the groaning masses already

35

there on the deck, determined to fight it out, impossible though the situation was.

The end was not long in coming. We had only been in our positions for a few minutes before we saw tanks making their way towards us from St Valéry. Ian and I manned the two Lewis guns but it was useless. His gun jammed after firing only a few rounds and mine would only fire single shots. When the tanks reached a point immediately above us they opened fire with their anti-tank guns. The first two shots landed on the shingle near the keel, throwing a shower of pebbles and shell splinters over the deck. The third shot blew a great hole in the ship's side and the fourth landed right on the deck. Everyone was screaming and shouting. Then I lost consciousness.

When I came to, there were Germans everywhere. A splinter had hit my forehead and my eyes were blinded with blood. There was scarcely a man who had not been hit somewhere. Ian had a splinter through his cheek, Colin had a nasty gash above his left eye and the skipper of the ship had half of one of his legs blown off. Poor chap, only twenty-four hours earlier he had been safe in his home in England. Now he was badly wounded and, like the rest of us, a prisoner of war.

Chapter 2

The first moments of captivity were agonizing. The loud guttural voices of our captors, their swagger and arrogance and perhaps above all their smart turn-out, which compared so noticeably with our own pitiful appearance, increased our natural despair. Their first concern seemed to be to discover if any of us had any valuable possessions. My field glasses and compass, which I had not thought of trying to hide, were seized upon with great delight by a large German corporal. After a search we were hustled together in a miserable group on the promenade while they tried to round up any stragglers who were still hiding amongst the rocks. A few tried to resist but they were soon pulled out of their hiding places and driven down to join us at the point of a bayonet with a great deal of swearing and cursing.

I was glad to say that a lot of trouble was taken at this stage with the wounded. The German medical orderlies were as considerate as our own would have been and there was a much appreciated issue of water. What with one thing and another we were still on the beach at four o'clock in the afternoon when we saw our boat lift off the sands with the incoming tide. It was a small comfort as she was now only a hulk and would never have got us back to England. Then we were formed into squads and marched up the cliff to where a further party of Germans awaited us with trucks for the wounded.

I can remember very little of the next three or four

hours. I started off with a walking party but found it difficult going as I had to hold a large cotton wool swab to my eyes and had such a dreadful headache that I hardly knew what I was doing. When the Germans discovered that I could not walk straight they put me in one of the trucks, where I passed out for a second time.

When I came to it was to find that I was in some sort of temporary hospital in what had once been a casino-type hotel at Forges les Eaux, many miles inland. The squalor was quite appalling. We were packed together cheek by jowl. The French wounded were in row upon row on the floor of an old theatre, the British were crowded five each into balcony boxes originally designed to accommodate two seats. I do not know whose lot was the more miserable. The straw on which we lay was filthy and the smell of festering wounds almost unbearable. Medical supplies were virtually non-existent and, although we were fortunate in having three British medical orderlies, there was little they could do for us.

When I had been there a little time and the bleeding had stopped, I joined others in trying to make a nominal roll of our own people. This was extremely difficult as many had strayed amongst the French contingent and others were so badly mutilated that it was hard to recognize them. Downstairs I found an old friend, Toby Tailyour, a Seaforth, who had a very bad shoulder wound which was becoming gangrenous and, near to him, our gallant ship's captain whose leg was so badly mauled that it was obvious that it would have to be amputated if his life was to be saved. He was extraordinarily cheerful and brought a lump to my throat when he apologized for not getting us off.

Perhaps worst of all was the food—or rather the lack of it. The cooking was done by some French soldiers on field cookers in the garden and there were possibly enough rations for a hundred whereas we numbered almost a thousand. Our ration was one very small meal a day of cold stew barely sufficient to cover the bottom of a soup plate. It was soon obvious to all of us that we would have to fend for ourselves or starve. Fortunately we were able to make friends with the French caretaker and his wife and through them we managed to buy odd extras with our few remaining francs, which happily had not been taken from us. I had not had either the chance or the foresight to collect cigarettes, which being a smoker added to my personal discomfort. I shall always remember the kindness of an R.A.S.C. driver who had been more provident and who generously shared his stock amongst the rest of us.

On 17 June, the fifth day of our incarceration, three British doctors arrived and they at once set to work on the worst cases. They had managed to open some sort of an operating theatre in a clinic nearby and they worked night and day. One thing that nobody could combat was the filth of our surroundings and the men soon became apathetic. However much the Germans cursed and however much we tried to keep them up to the mark they became daily more lethargic and careless about their personal cleanliness.

It was a great relief when we learned after a week that those of us who were less seriously wounded were to be moved to one of the main transit prison camps. After a short journey in an open truck we arrived at a field in which some four thousand prisoners were already collected. What a dreadful lot they looked! At least in the hospital there were washing facilities for those who chose to use them. These men looked as if they had not seen water for weeks. The clothes they wore were in rags and a travesty of a uniform. Many had appropriated articles of civilian clothing to maintain a semblance of decency. Some wore old straw hats, others ladies' felt ones. All had dented tin plates, mugs and saucepans hung around their waists like an ironmonger's shop. It was not long before I too became one of those raggle-taggle tramps.

We were drawn up in a winding column with German guards spaced at wide intervals along its length. I think the Germans took even fewer precautions in 1940 than did the Allies six months later when escorting the Italian prisoners in the North African desert. Apart from us British they had thousands of Frenchmen on their hands, so it was hardly surprising.

It was when I saw the shortage of guards, escorting us that the first thoughts of escaping entered my head.

We started in our trek eastwards, further and further from home and deeper and deeper into Europe with our final destination some bleak wire enclosure in the centre of Germany.

Soon the days fell into a routine. We were kicked into wakefulness just before dawn. Then we filed past a huge urn of tepid ersatz black coffee, holding out such receptacles as we could muster—a sardine or a cigarette tin. Perhaps we got a piece of black bread, perhaps not. After that the day's march began. There were no regular halts but every two or three hours the German guards would get tired of riding their bicycles and we would be allowed to fall out for a few minutes. The column was about four miles long and was preceded by a lorry with mounted machine-guns while another brought up the rear which was generally full of men who had fallen out on the march and could go no further. Each camp consisted of an open field where we covered ourselves with such bedding in the way of blankets and odd rags we had salvaged on the way as we could carry. Thus the stronger amongst us, could carry the heavier load, slept the more comfortably.

The only meal served besides the meagre breakfast was

when we stopped for the night and this was the cause of great bitterness amongst the British contingent. All the cooking was done by the French and they refused to feed us until all their own people had been served. As rations were extremely short this meant that we never got our fair share and we began to hate our allies intensely. On the other hand French civilians on the route often tried to hand out food to us, showing no partiality to their own country-men, which did something to reconcile us. After all it was a case of every man for himself and no doubt British troops would have acted the same as the French if the roles had been reversed.

Sanitation was non-existent. At each stopping place a part of the field was roped off for the functions of nature. Shallow trenches were dug and long wooden logs were erected horizontally on low struts, on which we were expected to straddle. Squatting next to an unhappy constipated warrior on one occasion, when I was successfully doing my "duty", he commented "Oh, you lucky bugger!" We were thankful when at last we could fall asleep, four of us huddled under one blanket.

At one staging camp we caught up with an earlier column and shared the site for one night. There must have been eight thousand of us altogether. I went in search of any of my own regiment who might be found with the first column. It was like looking for a friend at a Wembley Cup Final but to my joy I came across three of our signallers and they in turn led me to a group of about fifty Camerons. It was a shock to see these men whom I knew as smart, keen soldiers reduced to such vagrant conditions, but meet-ing up with them gave me great joy and I think they too were pleased to see me. They were wonderfully cheery and we spent a very happy hour or two together exchanging stories of our adventures. Realizing that I had no tobacco many of them pooled their resources and, in spite of my protests, insisted that I take a supply away with me.

The first time I really had a chance of making serious plans to escape was when we reached the staging camp at Doullens where, for the first time, we slept under cover. For some reason we were allowed to stay there for four days and during that time I began to recover some of my strength, both mentally and physically.

At Doullens the officers were for the first time separated from the men. There were only four British initially of whom Colin Hunter who had been with me from the beginning was one. Now the wound above his eye was beginning to swell up and cause him a lot of pain and he was taken to see a doctor. It was discovered that he still had a large piece of shell splinter under the skin and he had to be hospitalized. Thus I lost my closest friend of those days although we were later to meet up again under quite extraordinary circumstances. After a couple of days in Doullens we were soon joined by some more British officers from the Lothian and Border Horse and the Artillery, notably Fred Corfield and Johnnie Buckingham, both gunner officers who became particularly close friends.

Apart from the opportunity it gave us to discuss escape, Doullens was an unhappy transit camp. The French were being more infuriating than usual over food. The cooks were keeping back rations from us to sell to their comrades and the atmosphere became ugly in consequence. They were also running a black market in looted British cigarettes, charging as much as thirty-five shillings for a packet of twenty. One thing led to another until early one morning matters came to a head with our troops rushing the barricades between them and the French. The Germans who restored order were not unduly disturbed. One of them even remarked to us afterwards: "Of course your real enemies are the French, not us." It was clever propaganda.

In spite of this friction, however, we were quite sorry to leave Doullens and resume our marching routine. There was now an alteration in the arrangements whereby the officers were made to march in a group in the rear. We were also allowed to stand near the coffee machine when the morning issue was being made, which gave us an opportunity of encouraging our men as they filed past.

A most touching incident occurred at the start of our march from the Doullens fort. Out of a group of soldiers shuffling past, there stepped the figure of a diminutive Jock. With great delight I recognized him as my batman, Murdo Shand, whom I had not seen since the beach at St Valéry. He raised his arm in salute to his battered straw hat and, taking a packet from his haversack, handed it to me. "These are your washing things, Sir. I have been carrying them around with me in the hope of seeing you again," he said. Then he passed on in the jostling crowd and I never saw him again. I was so touched I practically burst into tears.

Fred, Johnnie and I had decided that we would stick together from now on and look out for an opportunity to get away. The trouble was that, marching at the rear of the column, we were immediately in front of the German lorry with its machine-guns pointing at our backs. We bitterly regretted that we had identified ourselves as officers and so brought this unwelcome close supervision.

Worse was to follow. The Germans suddenly insisted that we ride in a truck. This not only made surveillance more intense but it filled us with guilt that we should be riding while our men were struggling along on foot. Far more of them were now dropping out from exhaustion, fainting by the wayside or sitting nursing their blistered feet. There were so many of them that the Germans for the most part left them where they lay, no doubt to be picked up later. None of them had either the spirit or the physical strength to try and escape.

The whole column now stretched for miles and it was a woeful sight. Our trucks drove up and down alongside it but most of the men were too wretched even to look up as we passed. When we passed through the village of Frévent the local inhabitants, warned of our arrival, lined the roadway holding out food and drink. The men, not far from starvation, fought like animals for this manna from heaven, often spilling much of what they managed to grab.

The next camp was on a small racecourse on the outskirts of St Pol and for the first time we British were separated from the French. Here a most unfortunate incident occurred. As the British contingent entered the camp the cooks, German this time, were already busy at their stoves preparing the evening meal. The sight was too much for some of our starving men. Suddenly a large group of them broke ranks and made a rush for the cooking area. Those behind jostled those in front and in the ensuing confusion several of the stoves with their precious contents were knocked over. The men were only brought to their senses by the German guards firing over their heads.

I was immediately sent for by the commandant. As the senior British officer I was now given a severe lecture on the need to maintain discipline. It would have been easier to take if I had not found that he was a fair-minded German able to understand that we British were being driven to a state of desperation. He made it quite clear, however, that this sort of conduct would not be tolerated and that it could only lead to more severe security precautions and the stopping of civilians offering us food.

It was quite obvious that I must try to do something to improve morale and conduct and the only way I felt I could do this was by calling the men together and giving them a "pep" talk. It was not a task I looked forward to. I would have to lay down the law to a crowd who were near to breaking point and few of them were from my own unit. Obviously my sympathies were with them and not with the Germans yet somehow in their own interest I had to get across to them what the Commandant had told me with English-speaking Germans listening.

I called a meeting that night. My audience was large and when I started to speak there was no sound to be heard but my own very nervous voice. They listened to every word I had to say in hushed silence so that when I started to call for good behaviour I could not tell how it was being received. It came as a great relief, therefore, to be greeted, when I had finished, with a cheer. Just the same when I crawled under my blanket that night I was very depressed knowing how little I could do to help my countrymen.

From time to time Jocks of my battalion would come to me in the darkness and ask about means of escape. One of them was an Inverness man whom I had known particularly well before the war. Like all the others he had all manner of bright ideas as to how to get away but no idea of where to get away to. What most of the men wanted was leadership. They had the guts to try and escape but not the imagination to see very much further than simply getting away. Many of them wanted me to lead a group but I had to explain that such a course would be fatal. To escape successfully it would be necessary to live off the land and this was quite impossible if the party numbered more than two or three at the most. Thus there was very little I could offer but encouragement while I went ahead with my own selfish private plans.

It was on the next day that Fred, Johnnie and I decided to make our bid for freedom. We were once more allowed to join the main marching column and we felt it was a case of now or never. It was a misty morning. Shortly after leaving St Pol we turned to talk to two Gordon Highlanders who had been marching behind us only to discover that they were no longer there. This more than anything strengthened our determination to break for it.

About two hours after the start of the march, at about 8 am, we came to a roadway which was lined on either side by high hedges, rather like a Devonshire lane. This we felt was our moment. There was one guard wheeling his bicycle about five hundred yards ahead and another almost twice that distance behind. Johnnie watched the guard in the front and Fred the one behind while I looked out for a gap in the hedge. We made one dash for the hedge only to find it impossible to get through and managed to rejoin the column without being noticed by the guards. A few minutes later we made another try and this time we were successful. We went through a gap, tumbling on top of one another in our haste and then lay on our tummies scarcely daring to breathe while the column went on shuffling past.

We must have lain there for an hour before the end of the procession went by and we were able to raise our heads and take stock of our surroundings. We found we were in a meadow a few hundred yards from a farmhouse. There was an old woman moving about at the far side of the field. There had been previous occasions when we had heard that escapees had been given up to the Germans by the French so, although we would have to trust to their patriotism sooner or later, we preferred it to be later. We had with us a few hardly saved rations so we moved cautiously to a nearby cornfield and shared a tin of bully beef, intending to lie up until nightfall.

I cannot adequately describe our feelings in those first few hours of freedom. There was certainly no exultation and no heady optimism, rather the reverse. We felt now that every man's hand was against us and that we were little better off than escaping criminals. The pains we took to cover our traces were almost ludicrous. We went to great trouble to see that there were no flattened cornstalks and when two aeroplanes flew lazily overhead we were quite convinced that they were looking for us and crouched low in our cover, fearful that they would spot our white faces.

It was still early in the morning but the sun gradually rose higher and higher and it turned into a scorching hot day. Determined to move only by night we had to endure eight hours of intense discomfort, being broiled like lobsters as we lay sheltered from any breeze in the tall corn, ekeing out our precious water supply.

From the signs we had passed on the road we knew that we had been on the road to Bethune, past the junction branching to Lillers, and it was our plan to strike in a north-westerly direction towards the coast in the hope of finding a boat to take us across the Channel. It was not much of a plan but better than nothing. Fortunately Fred had somehow managed to retain his compass, which was just as well as our joint knowledge of navigation by the stars was non-existent.

By the time dusk came we were getting much more used to the idea of freedom and set off on our first night's cross country journey with confidence. It was hard going. Although the ground was perfectly flat we were constantly obstructed by thick bramble-entwined hedges and, to add to our troubles, a heavy dew came down soaking us as we walked. In all we could only have covered nine or ten miles before day started to break.

To our delight we came across a little clear-running stream where we buried our faces in the cold water and drank our fill. Soon afterwards we sighted a beautiful little hamlet surrounded by trees and, as it was now nearly full daylight, proceeded with greater caution.

It is an extraordinary thing that the more one tries to be quiet when moving across country, the greater the noise one seems to make. We were almost tip-toeing our way forward but every now and again one of us would stand on a twig and it would crack with a noise that sounded to us like a rifle shot. We were still a considerable distance from a farmhouse on the outskirts of the village when a dog started barking and went on for fully twenty minutes. We could not help laughing. For all our precautions there was no fooling that dog.

As the sun started to rise we lay up about forty yards from the farmhouse and held a short conference. It was possible that there were Germans billeted in the village or indeed in the farmhouse itself and all we could do was to wait and see. If the coast seemed clear we decided to knock on the door and take our chance.

It was about nine o'clock before we summoned enough courage to creep forward and when we knocked a further three dogs broke into a chorus of barking. There were sounds of movement inside and a moment later the door was opened by an elderly lady. She took one look at the apparitions who stood before her and slammed the door in our faces. We nearly bolted, but hearing her calling to someone else in the house, plucked up courage and stood our ground.

After what seemed an eternity the door was opened, this time by a younger woman who looked us over quickly and signalled to us to step inside. Both women stared at us with frightened eyes as we explained in our stumbling French who we were and what we wanted. It was obvious that they did not much like the situation and I cannot

4 The author as 'Pierre' when hiding with the Mailles.

5 Colin Hunter, the 4th Camerons' Intelligence Officer.

6 John Buckingham, the author's companion from Doullens to Marseilles.

7 The wine merchant and his wife, M and Mme Vaubeck, with whom the author and Johnnie spent their first night after escaping from Tournai.

really blame them, for we later learned that the Germans had issued the most fearful warnings as to what would happen to anyone found assisting prisoners to escape.

To their credit they did not turn us out but indicated that we could lie up for the day in the loft above the pig-house, and in the meantime gave us a little food.

The day was wearing on when Fred had what we thought was a good idea. Why not send for the village curé and ask his help? It might be expected that the Church would at least be neutral and able to offer us some good advice. Obligingly the younger woman went in search of him and towards nightfall he arrived. He proved to be an elderly man with grey hair and a face lined with worry. He could make no suggestions for our future movements and pro-fessed not to know if there were any Germans in the area. It was obvious that he was even more frightened than our involuntary hostesses and he soon left us. Before he went, however, he awkwardly pressed a very acceptable sand-wich into each of our hands.

Just before we were due to move on, we were given some hot soup and managed to buy two tins of herrings and some bread. We also saw a ridiculously small, badly scarred pocket-handkerchief of a map of the North of France on the wall and, on showing interest, were willingly given it. It was so tiny that when the hairline of the compass was laid on it, it obscured two or three villages, but it was better than nothing.

That next night was no better than the first. The country was now more undulating but this had the advantage that we could pick out landmarks on the skyline by the thin light of the moon, which saved a great deal of compass reading. On the other hand the country was closer with a number of steep banks to negotiate, down which we some-times slithered dangerously. From time to time, too, we

49

woud come suddenly upon livestock which frightened us as we thought they were human beings.

Just before dawn we approached another farm, again only to be greeted by a storm of barking from a number of small dogs. It was still too early to expect the inhabitants to be up and about so we sought refuge in an adjoining barn where we lay down on some sacks to await daylight.

Eventually we pulled ourselves together and went forward to knock at the door. Our approach was heralded by a cackling of chickens and barking of dogs which stretched our nerves to breaking point. The moment the door opened, however, we knew we were in luck. With a quick gesture the lady of the house beckoned us inside and took charge of us as if we were her children.

There is no praise high enough for Monsieur and Madame Pouilly. Madame in particular waited for no explanations but quickly set about getting us a meal while her husband, a small, kindly looking man, hovered in the background smiling a welcome and nodding vigorously when we caught his eye.

What a meal! We had six fried eggs each and limitless quantities of bread and butter, followed by a huge bowl of fresh strawberries and a great jug of cream. It was so long since we had eaten a decent meal that an air of unreality descended on the whole proceedings. We simply ate and ate until even we could manage no more. Then Madame Pouilly indicated that we should go upstairs to sleep. She put us in one enormous bed covered over with eiderdowns and we knew what it felt like to be in heaven. In a few seconds we were all three fast asleep.

We felt we had scarcely closed our eyes however when we were jerked into wakefulness again by Madame Pouilly shaking us violently. Some German motorcyclists had come to the house and were now sitting in the parlour which we had so recently vacated. Madame Pouilly was, however, equal to the occasion. She bundled us out of the back window and led us to the loft in one of the nearby barns where we spent the rest of the day, too tired to care if the whole German army were to come upon us. We had two more great meals that day, carried out to us in a basket by Madame Pouilly. That woman was absolutely intrepid. She did not have a trace of fear of the Germans, only a bitter hatred built up in two wars and a determination to do all that she could to thwart them.

Johnnie remembered that he had met some rich people who lived in the neighbourhood before the war and M. Pouilly, later in the day, was sent off to try and contact them. When he returned it was to tell us that he had been unable to find them. Instead he had gone round his own friends and collected for us a quantity of peasant's clothing which we now tried on amidst much laughter.

All too soon it was time for us to move on. We were supplied with quantities of food to take with us, sacks in which to put our newly-gained clothes, as we had a fear that if we were caught wearing civilian clothes we might be taken for spies and, almost best of all, two warm blankets apiece. This encounter cheered us up more than anything had done since the beginning of the disastrous retreat. A place ought to be reserved in heaven for such people as the Pouillys.

Before we left we learned that, although very little was known about the general position, there had been sounds of shell fire from the Boulogne area and it was generally rumoured that the British were once again fighting on French soil. Whilst this was not true, it gave us great encouragement at the time and made us determined to redouble our efforts to get to the coast quickly.

With ample food for several days we now had to take

no more immediate risks in calling at farmhouses and we took to the life of tramps with relish. Johnnie turned out to be an excellent cook. We sited our fires carefully in the middle of woods so that the trees would dissipate the smoke and lessen the risk of discovery and sampled the stews and soups he produced with as much enjoyment as if we had been dining at the Savoy.

Our burdens were now heavier and consequently we made less progress during the short hours of darkness each night. Also we reckoned that, as we drew nearer to the coast, we would be more likely to run into German troops and took greater precautions accordingly. The most trying part, in spite of the lack of physical effort involved, was the lying up during the hours of daylight. We had to spend almost sixteen hours at a stretch, virtually without movement and sleep did not come easily as our minds would not relax. We were always thankful when darkness came and we could move on.

On the fourth night we lost ourselves completely. Soon after we started we came up against a large wood and decided to strike right to get round it. Unfortunately this was a bad decision. Coming to what we thought was the corner of the wood, we found it continued to slope backwards, necessitating a further detour. That wood seemed endless and we were forced further and further right until we were frightened of losing our bearings altogether. We turned sharp left but again our way was blocked so we spent the night see-sawing backwards and forwards and making no progress whatsoever. Eventually at four in the morning, we gave it up as a bad job and lay down to sleep.

When daylight came we discovered that we had travelled in a large loop and finished up near our starting point. It was a sad exhibition of compass-reading. We changed tactics and took a new and bold decision. We decided that we would risk wearing our civilian clothes, which would enable us to move occasionally by daylight as well as by night. We cooked and ate the last of our food supplies and, dressed as French peasants, plunged into the wood, looking for a clearing on some high ground from which we could get our bearings.

It was not long before we found what we were looking for. We were nearer the far edge of the wood than we had thought and soon found ourselves looking down on a village and beyond it miles and miles of open land stretching away to the north-west. It was a very cheering moment.

We studied the village for some time and seeing few signs of life decided that we could take the risk and investigate it further. It had a long street wth cottages spaced some way apart from each other on either side. By great good fortune we discovered that the only village store was at our end of the street. It seemed to be one of those shops that contained everything from a hairpin to a rasher of bacon and we stood watching from a short distance for some time as villagers came and went, buying what they wanted and waiting to gossip for a minute or two before going on their way. At the same time we took stock of one another. Johnnie's trousers reached scarcely below the knee while mine were so tight in the crutch that I could scarcely walk. Only Fred's suit fitted him passably well. Unkempt and unshaven we were more like a comic trio in a stage act than the French peasants we were supposed to be.

I doubt if we would have had the courage to enter that shop if it had not been that, as we stood looking at each other, the proprietress spotted us and together with one or two shoppers came bustling out to collect us. It did not add one little bit to our self-confidence that no one had the slightest doubt what we were. Fortunately they were the kindest of people.

53

Soon there was quite a little crowd gathered round who pressed all manner of goods upon us and we had the greatest difficulty in paying. Not only the shopkeeper but her customers pressed things upon us and we finished up with quite a few additions to our wardrobe. Johnnie was given an old blue beret which he treasured for a long time, Fred got a cloth cap and I was given a black peaked fisherman's hat such as is worn by many in that part of France. Whilst we still looked dishevelled, our new purchases really helped us look our parts.

We had not been long in the shop when two girls entered, one of whom spoke quite good English. She told us that there was a small beach a little north of Le Touquet where we would find some boys who would hire us canoes to cross the Channel. The thought of crossing the Channel in a canoe appalled us but the girl explained that the term meant anything up to a fair-sized dinghy. We were also interested to learn that four other Britishers had recently passed through the village on their way to the coast. This gave us considerable heart and we congratulated ourselves on having had the courage to venture abroad in daylight.

At the same time we were advised to avoid any dense woods. It appeared that there had been many Senegalese troops brought over for the defence of France and in the retreat they had taken to the woods still armed with their rifles and quite unable to understand what had happened to them. They had now formed themselves into bands, lying up in dense cover during the hours of daylight, ravaging the countryside at night by breaking into isolated farms and generally behaving like packs of wolves. They had no compunction in shooting anyone who crossed their paths and were hunted by friend and foe alike.

We estimated that we were still some twenty five miles from the coast and for the next few days and nights we made steady progress, avoiding all buildings and contact with people and choosing our sleeping places with great care.

On the eighth night (1/2 July) we got over-confident and did not give ourselves enough time to find a suitable place to lay up. As dawn broke we found we had nearly walked into a small village, so turned sideways and rapidly made our way up a nearby wooded hill. As we climbed the slope we heard a raucous voice issuing orders quite close by and found ourselves looking down on the courtyard of a chateau, not a hundred yards away, in which German soldiers were drilling. It was a nasty moment and we made a dash for the dense cover of the trees where we lay up like mice for the rest of the day.

The next night we got away as early as we could and covered more ground than usual. Just before dawn we came to a wide stream which luckily had a small bridge crossing it nearby. We wore battledress by night and had already got soaked wading another stream earlier and had no desire to repeat the experience and lie in wet clothes all day. It was a risk worth taking so we changed into our French gear and walked boldly over the bridge. Seeing a farm close by we decided, with unusual brashness, to ask them for help and information. As we approached we noticed a pair of civilians sitting in a smart Peugeot car outside the door staring at us. We did not like the look of them but we could not turn back so we asked them if there were any Germans in the district.

"The place is full of Germans," the man growled. Then he looked at us a bit more closely. "You're British aren't you! Now you just clear off or I'll put the Germans on to you. We want nothing to do with you!"

"Yes, get out of here," shouted his wife. "We are decent people. Go away!"

They certainly were an unpleasant couple and we wanted to tell them what we thought of them but we had no doubt that they meant what they said and that they would not hesitate to contact the Germans. Without more ado we made ourselves scarce, cursing ourselves for being so rash.

In trying to find a suitable hiding place for the day we climbed one more wooded hill and, coming to the crest, looked down the other side. Spread before us, the waves glinting in the morning sunshine, was the English Channel! Moses viewing the promised land could not have been more excited than we were.

All that day we lay in the bushes gazing down at the sea. Before us the hill dropped steeply to a tarmac road and beyond that the ground continued flat for about two miles to the water's edge. A wide river estuary ran in from the left and by it lay quite a large town. We soon realized that it must be Le Touquet—the playground of the rich British before the war, and the estuary was the Canche running up to Etaples. We wondered what they would say now if we walked into the Bristol or the Westminster to book a room or started to play a round on the golf course.

We had not been far out in our reckonings and from our map we knew that our objective, St Cecile, lay a short distance north along the coast. We felt that it might just be possible to pick up a boat in the estuary in front of us and therefore kept it under close observation. All day little sailing boats glided about in the bay, sometimes coming in to tie up on the bank for an hour or so. If only one of them would be left there overnight! For a long time we discussed whether an object lying in some rushes straight ahead of us was a boat or not. "It is a boat," said Johnnie. "No, it's not," said Fred, "I am sure it is," I said. "No, definitely it is not," said Johnnie, and in the end we had to admit that it was too shapeless to be a boat. The trouble was that we were wishing too hard for a miracle.

We soon noticed that none of the sailing boats ventured as far as the sea itself and after watching them for some time we realized why. From the seaward end of some sheds built on the promontory, the noses of two evil-looking guns protruded. It was obvious that to sail beyond the riverbanks was forbidden and that any boat doing so would have to run the gauntlet of their fire.

By five o'clock all the boats had disappeared up the river again towards Etaples and we could see that our only hope was the beach at St Cecile. We planned to move north that night, keeping about five miles inland to miss the German beach defence posts. There was evidence of the Germans everywhere. At one point we came across a number of temporarily laid telephone wires running inland from the coast and obviously used for military purposes. The temptation to cut them was almost irresistible but we realized that we would do no damage that could not be quickly repaired and would probably only call down the wrath of the authorities on innocent heads, so we desisted.

That night we had a good splash around naked in a clear running stream outside the little village of Dannes and, greatly refreshed, made our way to a wood on the edge of the sand dunes about a mile from the sea. On the way we passed several notice boards which announced in English "DANGER—RANGES". It made us feel very homesick as these were the rifle charges used by the B.E.F. only a few months before.

Early in the morning we came across an isolated farmhouse and, thinking it deserted, decided to break in and see what we could find. To our horror, we found that it was inhabited. An old woman greeted us at the door and told us that it was a soldiers' billet but that fortunately they were out. She was a brave and kindly soul. We could not stay there but she insisted that we have something to eat and drink and warned us about the German garrison in the neighbourhood. There was, she told us, a very strict curfew along the whole coast of France and that we would be well advised to trust to our disguises and move about only in daylight.

Shortly afterwards, we almost ran into a group of about a dozen Germans doing rifle practice and stole back quietly into the wood where, exhausted, we soon fell asleep. It was three o'clock before we awoke and, taking the old woman's advice, set out to reconnoitre for a boat before it got too late.

Carrying our sacks on our back we looked more than ever like three down and outs but we were full of confidence. About half a mile to our left we spotted some people moving about, but whether French or German we could not tell. When we got down to the beach we started out on to the sand but Johnnie suddenly stopped us in our tracks. He had spotted a party of men walking towards us. We dived for cover into the dunes and about fifteen Germans led by an officer passed by only a few yards away. Worse, we soon spotted a sentry standing looking out to sea and realized that the coast was being very carefully watched. Our chances of finding a boat were remote and our chances of getting away if we did find one, even more slim. Nonetheless we determined to press on to St Cecile for we still had a childish hope that what the girl had told us in the shop a few days ago might just be true.

We reached St Cecile around 4 pm. The place was lined with derelict bathing chalets and on investigating one we found that it had been completely ransacked. From behind some old lace curtains we looked out on to a rough gravel road leading down to the sea and noticed that there was a cafe right opposite which still appeared to be doing business. Now we had to decide on our immediate movements. Johnnie and I were all for venturing over to it, despite our ten days' growth of beard and filthy appearance. Fred advised greater caution but it was two to one so, leaving Fred to guard our hiding place, we walked boldly across the road.

The proprietress of the cafe immediately guessed our identity and could scarcely speak for her agitation. She told us that the coastguard station was only thirty yards up the road and that the place was guarded day and night. Furthermore she thought all the Channel coast was closely guarded. The nearest village was Camiers about a mile and a half down the road. We bought some chocolate and chewing gum and quickly left.

Desperately disappointed, we realized that our journey had been completely wasted. The chances of finding, and getting away in, a boat were nil. There was nothing for it we felt but to retrace our steps and to try and make our way across the whole of France to the Mediterranean, however long it might take. So far we had only travelled about forty miles and it had taken us nine days, so the prospect was intimidating.

In retrospect all I can say now was that at this point Johnnie and I took leave of our senses. For days we had crept like hunted animals across country, avoiding all contact with people unless it was completely necessary. Now, surrounded by our enemies, we did not return to our chalet but set off boldly for Camiers in broad daylight. We passed a church and saw three or four Germans scanning the horizon from the tower but still we kept on. We had left our sacks with Fred and now only carried a small bread bag which had been given us a few days earlier.

We soon struck the main Dannes–Le Touquet road and

turned right towards Camiers. We had not gone far when we passed some German horse lines in a field by the road. Suddenly a German sentry stepped out in front of us and demanded our papers. It was a dreadful moment. With our hearts in our mouths we started to gesticulate in what we thought was a typical French manner to indicate that we had come from Dannes and had left our papers behind. We even threw in a few words in execrable French. It was indeed fortunate that he had apparently no knowledge of the language. When we had finished we stood for some moments just looking at one another, neither side knowing quite what to do next. Then he made a gesture which seemed to indicate that we should accompany him down the road and we completely gave up hope. It was only when we set off and found that he was not following us that we realized that we had been let go. That German sentry was an incredibly stupid individual.

Instead of inspiring us to greater caution, this incident added to our confidence and we strode into Camiers as if we owned the place. There was a grocer's shop on the left and we entered and asked for some bread. The lady looked at us curiously and demanded if we were not aware that coupons were required for bread and that we should go to the bread store. This we did and managed to persuade a young boy to go in for us and see what he could do. He came out with two loaves without coupons. We then entered another shop and bought some tins of fish.

Returning the way we came, we again passed the grocer's shop and this time the woman came out to greet us. Taking us into a back room she explained that she knew just what we were but that she had not dared to let on when we had first passed as there had been too many people about. It appeared that the Germans had killed her husband a few days earlier and now all she wanted was revenge. Filling our haversacks with food, this brave woman kissed us on both cheeks and sent us on our way with her blessing. We felt that we had been, not lucky, but extremely clever.

As we walked back German soldiers, laughing and shouting, passed us to and fro on bicycles. They took no notice and when we came to the spot where we had been stopped by the sentry there was no sign of him. Everything was going our way.

At the road junction we turned gaily into the track leading down to our chalet where we had left Fred, got past the look-out tower and were within twenty yards of our destination when we noticed that we were being followed by a man on horseback. When he caught up with us we saw with horror that he was a German officer. He rode past us and we continued on our way but he had not ridden ten yards by when he wheeled his horse round and stopped us. He was a big, fat lout of a man, the type of German officer you often see portrayed on films. He started to shout at us, asking us who we were and what we were doing. I did the best I could with my French but he was a persistent character and obviously not satisfied. We knew there was a German post close by and on his shouted order three soldiers came running out and surrounded us. One of them was a fluent French speaker and the game was up.

All our efforts had been in vain and we were prisoners once more. We had certainly learnt one lesson the hard way and should have listened to the more cautious Fred.

Chapter 3

When it dawned on the soldiers who surrounded us that they had captured two British officers their delight knew no bounds. They tore at our clothes, searching us roughly and snatching anything whether of value or not. Then it started to rain and our captors returned to their guard hut one at a time and came back wearing British gas capes. As we had carried these beastly things all over the north of France with strict instructions that they must not be used for their only possible function of keeping out the rain, it now thoroughly annoyed me to see them being worn by the enemy.

While all this was going on we were very conscious of the fact that poor Fred, cooped up in our chalet, was watching the whole pantomime and must have seen us walk into the trap. Before leaving him we had agreed that, if we were captured, we should disclose our hiding place and all stick together. When the Germans heard there was another one of us, they became very excited and, drawing their revolvers, rushed our hiding place as if they were mounting a major attack. The unresisting Fred was led out in triumph with three revolvers pointing at the small of his back. Very sensibly he had taken advantage of the breathing space to dress in his battledress and he brought our sacks out with him to establish our bona fides as British officers.

The fat oaf of a German officer had remained seated on

his horse. Now that it was established that we carried no arms he became very brave and, ordering us to hang on to his stirrup leathers, set off for his headquarters with us trotting ignominiously beside him. How I hated him sitting up there like a sack of potatoes, gloating over his triumph.

During our travels I had, very stupidly, as I could now see, kept a record of our experiences. Fortunately it had not been found when I was being searched but now obviously I had to get rid of it. It would be bad for us if they discovered that we had already escaped once as they would guard us the more closely. I now had it screwed up in my hand and, passing over a small stream, I managed to flip it into the water unseen.

News of our capture had spread rapidly and as we passed knots of spectators gathered to watch the discomfiture. It took us about an hour to reach the local Headquarters at Dannes. As we passed through the gates we were witnesses to an unpleasant piece of Prussianism which showed that I was justified in taking such a dislike to our captor. The sentry sprang to attention at his approach but obviously not smartly enough for his liking. Dismounting he strode over to the wretched man and delivering a tirade of abuse, struck him a hard blow on the cheek with his open hand. The sentry never moved a muscle and his dignity showed up his persecutor for what he was—a blusterer and a bully.

The search at our point of capture had been more frenzied than thorough for we still had our little map as well as, most valuable of all, our compass. Now we learned that we were to be searched again individually and agreed to slip the compass and the map to each other during the search in the hope that they would not be discovered. We lost the map but mercifully the ruse worked over the compass. They took everything else off us including personal items such as my gold identity bracelet and all our carefully preserved food, except for some bread which we were told would be our rations for the rest of the day. Surprisingly, too, they left us with our civilian clothes.

Shortly after this a Captain arrived and he too wanted to question us. He was a podgy but kindly enough looking man with eyes which twinkled behind his pince-nez. He did not appear very interested in the whole affair until it came to a question as to where we had got our food. Stupidly we admitted that it was Camiers and at once he insisted that I, as the senior officer, should go with him in his car and point out the shop to him. It was quite obvious that it was considered a serious crime on the part of our friendly shopkeeper and that she would get into trouble if I identified her so I had to pretend that I could not recognize the store. We drove up and down the street for some time before he gave up, realizing that I was either too stupid or too stubborn to give him the information he wanted.

It was some time before we rejoined the others. We were motored to an attractive French villa on the hillside with a well-kept garden and obviously an altogether more important headquarters than the one at Dannes. Once more we were interrogated singly while the other two sat on a bench outside the interviewing room. I say "sat" but in fact every time an officer passed we were required to jump to our feet if we were to avoid a blow in the back with the butt of a rifle from the sentry who stood behind us.

We all stuck to our story that we had been wandering about ever since the fall of St Valéry and they had to be satisfied with that. The interrogation over for the time being, we were driven inland to Montreuil and locked up in a barred room in some barracks with a sentry permanently on duty outside the door.

We stayed in our cell for four days and the time did not pass unpleasantly. Our guards were ordinary German in-

8 The outside wall of the barracks at Tournai over which the author made his escape.

9 M and Mme Maille outside their farm in Ennevelin.

10 François and Michel Maille today.

fantry and not professional gaolers. They were friendly and only too anxious to discuss topical affairs with us. Even the officers were most polite and always saluted us before addressing us, in true Continental fashion. The unit had not seen much fighting but had brought up the rear, marching on their feet most of the way from Holland.

Of course they were all steeped in the doctrine of Hitler and firmly believed that they would soon overrun the British Isles. They had even been given the date for their entry into London—15 August, 1940.

We had one special friend, Hans, who was a clerk in the orderly room. He visited us every day and never failed to bring a packet of cigarettes. We asked him for writing paper which he brought in great quantities and offered to try and see that our letters were posted through the Red Cross. None of them ever arrived but I am sure that Hans did his best. This, of course, was one of our greatest worries. We were very conscious of the fact that we would have been reported missing and there could have been no record yet of our being prisoners of war. It was easy to imagine the anxiety which our families must be enduring and how overjoyed they would be to get any kind of news about us.

Hans went even further with his kindnesses. On the third evening he took us past the guard into his little office and switched on the wireless tuned into London. Alas, the news had just finished and all we heard was a speech by Lord Woolton on food control, but it was a brave and generous act.

The cooks, too, were very good to us and I think we fared better than the German soldiers, as we often received an extra portion when all the others had finished. Wonder of wonders, we even got real butter with our black bread. Our other problem was tobacco. We were all three smokers

5—RTSV * *

and the twenty cigarettes Hans brought us every day did not go far. One day we managed to attract the attention of an elderly French woman passing our cell window which overlooked the street and offered her our last hundred-franc note for some cigarettes. The good soul soon returned with four large bags of coarse smoking mixture together with numerous packets of papers for rolling cigarettes. Thereafter we had no more money but enough tobacco to last six months.

We were escorted to the wash-house where we shared the hot water with the troops, who were quick to lend us razors, soap etc. so that we could get rid of our now formidable beards. We felt so much better for this and for the opportunity of scrubbing our clothes that we resolved never again to go escaping without proper washing equipment. My kit so carefully kept and passed back to me by Murdo Shand in Doullens had long since disappeared.

In the middle of our stay we received another official visit, this time from a senior Intelligence Officer who was of quite a different calibre from our previous questioners. He had lived in London much of his life and spoke perfect English. He asked us details of our regiments, companies, batteries and so on but when we refused to answer replied very civilly that he was not going to press us to disobey our orders and disclose any military information. Instead, rather like a conjurer producing a rabbit out of a hat, he proceeded to tell each one of us exactly who we were and to give us the names and numbers of our units even down to troop level in the case of Johnnie and Fred. It astonished us at the time but in retrospect I suppose it was not too difficult for him as he had had most of the captured members of the 51st Division through his hands.

Having finished his interrogation he gave us full details of what life was to be like in a prison camp and asked us all manner of personal questions as to religion, next of kin and even what sort of games we liked to play. He then wished us good luck and gave it as his opinion that our captivity would not be a long one as the war would soon be over. It was a friendly and very polished performance.

Most of our time at Montreuil was spent watching the soldiers at work and play on the barrack square. It was very like a British barracks with weapon training going on in one corner and drill or some other activity in another. At every break they played football with much enthusiasm, which greatly excited our guards. We were allowed out to sit on our cell steps to watch.

There was only one individual with whom we were at loggerheads. This was a corporal who was full of arrogance and self-importance. He took great delight in showing us propaganda photographs in various magazines of retreating Allied troops and refugees. One day he was in charge of a parade right under our window. Three of his squad were late on parade and he went wild with rage. When they were brought out for punishment, he made them get down on their hands and knees and crawl pushing corks along with their noses in the dust. It was a nauseating sight.

We were almost sorry when the four days were up and we were told that we were to be moved. Since our arrival more British had been sent to the barracks so that there were about fifteen of us in all. The others had been visited by the Red Cross and amongst other things had a few old copies of the *Tatler* and the *Sketch*. It really made us quite angry to see pictures of people enjoying themselves in evening clothes in places like the Cafe de Paris and the Ritz.

This time our march was quite different from anything we had previously experienced. There was a guard to every two prisoners and there was no chance of escape. We had complained to the Intelligence Officer at Montreuil that we had had all our possessions taken from us which, to our surprise, made him both apologetic and angry. As a result of his intervention everything had been returned to us down to the bar of chocolate, except of course the map.

Our march continued inland to Hesdin and here we caught up with another contingent of prisoners, where sadly our friendly Regimental guards left us and we were taken over by the grim-faced P.O.W. professionals. Inevitably there now came another search and again we lost most of our things, this time, our precious civilian clothes. The only object of value to us which we still managed to keep was the compass. This was achieved by the astute Fred who slipped it under the instep of his boot and managed to retrieve it after the guards had passed him. A prisoner a few miles farther on was not so lucky. He was found in possession of a small marlin spike and a Verey light pistol and was immediately sentenced to solitary confinement.

Once more we were back to the appalling prison rations of dry bread and tepid coffee essence. We three were the sole British officers in the party and we were allotted an upper storey room to ourselves where the only amenity was some filthy straw in one corner. Again the chances of escape were minimal. We looked out of our window towards a thick forest some kilometres away. If only we could reach that we felt we would be able to lie up long enough to get away, but between us and freedom there was a space too wide to jump and the outside wall was twenty feet high. Regretfully we curled up on the straw and were soon asleep.

We could only have slept for an hour when we were awakened by the guard who told us that a German officer wanted to speak to us. We were surprised when a young Air Force captain came into our room and shook each of us warmly by the hand. We took to him immediately. It trans-

68

pired that he had an English wife from Ealing who was now living in Munich and who had asked him to make a point of keeping a friendly eye on any British he came across. He himself knew England well and we had a long chat about places and people. It made us very homesick. When he finally left he gave us each a packet of cigarettes and wished us all the best of luck. What a refreshing contrast to our sour German guards.

Next day, to our disgust, we learned that we were to be transported by lorry, which cut out any chance of getting away. The lorry was covered and a guard sitting near the tail-board kept us under close observation. Sometimes we had the chance of peeping round the canopy to read the signposts and in this way discovered that we were driving along familiar roads in the St Pol area and soon we passed the very hole in the hedge through which we had crawled to temporary freedom a fortnight earlier.

About midday we entered the outskirts of a big town which we soon discovered to be Lille, whose fleshpots were well known to many of us earlier in the year in the phoney war phase. Rather to our amusement the driver lost his way and we spent some time driving round the suburbs in circles before coming to a dead end on a patch of waste ground which was being used as a collecting point for captured Allied guns. There must have been a thousand French 75's drawn up in ranks. They were all of 1914 vintage, quite out of date with wooden wheels, but it was still a sad sight.

It was some time before we eventually reached our billet for the night, which was another grim-looking barracks and it was here that for the first time we were required to fill in official prison forms. Hitherto we had simply been questioned for information of military value. Now we were being documented for our lives in a prison camp. The dreaded wire cage was drawing closer and closer and it was becoming all the more imperative that we should escape again soon before it became a reality.

We were in the Kléber Caserne and we British were looked after with particular strictness. The French were sent out in work parties every day but we were cooped up together, with no chance of joining them.

We met several other British prisoners, many with hard-luck escape stories. One which has stuck in my mind is of four escapees who actually managed to find a boat near Le Touquet and evade the guards. It had no engine but the oars were there and they thought it worth a try to row to England. After three days, by which time their hands were in ribbons from rowing, there was still no sight of land and they had been without water for twenty-four hours. Suddenly they spotted a British warship on the horizon and, summoning up the last of their strength, they rowed frantically towards it. Alas, it soon disappeared from view but then they saw land ahead. They made it with the last of their strength and were met on the beach by a German officer! They had rowed in a semi-circle and landed back in France near Boulogne. Their captors seemed genuinely sorry for them and gave them a good meal in the blockhouse over-looking the Channel. When they had eaten, one of the Germans beckoned them over and pointed to the warship they had chased, which had now moved into view again. "What bad luck for you all," the German Officer said sympathetically.

I was sad to see one day the two Gordon Highlanders who had escaped just before us from the line of march at St Pol being brought in and soon after them an old school friend of mine, Peter Grazebrook. All our talk was now of escape and every aspect of the problem was examined over and over again. One of the lucky things about the Kléber barracks was that the guards made no attempt to stop the local populace from passing food through the gates to us and we took every advantage of this situation to further our plans. Practically all our visitors were girls and Johnnie was certainly the Romeo of our party. He had had friends in Lille whom he had visited in peacetime and one of his fans was able to put him in contact with an old flame. Through her it was arranged for us to get some civilian clothes wrapped up in food parcels. It was a great triumph.

I myself was also able to make a little headway with the girls. My particular friend was a local school mistress whom I managed to talk to privately by climbing on to the roof of a low building abutting the perimeter wall when the sentries were out of sight. Together we evolved a rough plan of escape. It was very simple. We were to find a place where we could scale the wall at night. My friend would meet us outside and guide us to safety.

There followed a careful study of the walls. We had heard some of our predecessors had managed to escape over the roof of the shower-baths, but the Germans had discovered this weakness and it was now doubly guarded. The only thing to do was to wait for complete darkness and make a careful tour of inspection. We came across one or two scalable points but invariably our efforts were thwarted by passing sentries and in the end we had to give up the attempt. Next day we were told we were to be moved again.

When we climbed into the lorries a roll-call was taken and there was much excitement when it was discovered that one of our number was missing. He was a military policeman who had managed to join one of the French working parties outside the walls and slipped away. The Germans were furious but it raised our hopes.

Another day passed driving farther east. At midday

we crossed over the border into Belgium, which depressed us. We had been told that we could expect less help from the Belgian civilians than from the French.

We stopped that night in another high-walled barracks in Tournai. By great good luck there was a group of British waiting at the gate to see us arrive and to them we slipped our sacks containing our civilian clothing. It was just as well as we were now subjected to another search. After it was over, we picked up our precious belongings from our new friends. Again the walls were high and forbidding but near our billet we discovered a small hole about eighteen inches square, just large enough for a man to squeeze through. We watched it like cats, hoping for a chance to use it once darkness fell.

Whenever we arrived at a new prison, we made it an early priority to question those British who had been there for some time in the hope of picking up some useful information. At Tournai we discovered that there was a permanent party of British who had been kept there to do various chores. Apparently the Germans had asked for volunteers with mining experience and about a dozen had volunteered and then found to their dismay that what they had volunteered for was the disarming of British and French anti-tank mines strewn in great profusion around the countryside. However, they seemed to be quite resigned to their lot. In fact they were rather an apathetic bunch with no spirit at all. In particular there was a sergeant-major with whom we discussed the possibility of escape. To our disgust he quite blatantly advised us against any attempt on the grounds that it would only make matters worse for those left behind.

He told us that a few days before our arrival an infantry captain and an R.A.M.C. doctor had tried to escape and had been shot. He assured us that he had heard the machine-guns with his own ears and that later the Germans had told him: "You see what happens to anyone who tries to escape from here. Your friends are now very dead." It is lucky for him that I do not now remember his name or I would have made life very difficult for him. I was later to learn that what he told us was completely untrue.

There were now five of us determined to make an escape attempt; Johnnie, Fred and I together with my school friend Peter Grazebrook and a signals officer. Our hopes were set on the hole in the wall. We took it in turns to watch it when, just before dusk, a working party came along and carefully nailed it up. Once again our only chance was over the wall.

We had made a careful reconnaissance and discovered that there was a wash-house built against the outer wall with a flat roof which came to within two feet of the top. It seemed quite possible that we could lie on this roof and wait an opportunity to drop over the other side when the patrolling sentries were out of sight. At this stage the signaller volunteered to drop out. He thought that we would have a better chance working in two pairs and someone had to be the odd man out. It was an act of great self-sacrifice, particularly as he volunteered to help us as a look-out man right up to the moment when we could get away.

One hour after dark we collected our belongings and managed without great difficulty to climb on to the wash-house roof. There we kept watch in turn peering over the wall in the hope of catching the guards in an off moment. Johnnie kept us on tenter-hooks when he was not on watch by immediately falling asleep and snoring loudly. It was a long cold night and we thought that our chance was never going to come. Dawn broke and we were still trapped, but the roof was wide enough to conceal our whereabouts from anyone passing below.

We lay there all that day and all the following night. We

had now decided that, in view of the curfew, it would be better for us to put on our civilian clothes and move by daylight. We could not see any machine-gun posts and we discovered by day that the sentries made a complete circuit of the wall instead of a short lateral beat down each side. This meant that our area of wall was unobserved during each circuit for about five minutes. We drew lots on who should go first and the lot fell on Johnnie and me who were paired together. Fred and Peter were to follow two minutes later. We agreed to work separately so once again we drew lots for compass and a map that Peter had. Lots were cast and Fred and Peter won. To my surprise they chose the map.

We decided that whatever happened we would make our break early on the morning of 15 July. I did not sleep much that night, partly from excitement and partly from worrying about everything that might go wrong. The drop on the other side was about eighteen feet and viewed from where we crouched on the roof it seemed a long way down. Suppose one of us ricked an ankle? It seemed a very real possibility. We had been lucky with the people we had met on our last escape. Could we rely on being as lucky a second time?

Our chance came at 6.30 am, just as day was breaking. I was to go first. I lowered myself until my arms were fully stretched and I was only hanging on by my fingertips. Then, with my heart in my mouth, I let go. A moment later I hit the ground with a bone-jarring jolt and rolled clear. Johnnie followed immediately and he too landed safely. After the long tense hours of waiting and wondering, the elation of having overcome the first obstacle was overwhelming. Picking ourselves up we sprinted some fifty yards to a line of bushes and threw ourselves down behind them. There was no outcry and once more we were free.

Chapter 4

It was fortunate for us that the barracks at Tournai were on the outskirts of the town so that we were now faced with open fields instead of having to make our way through streets.

There were some peasants already at work in the fields but they took no notice of us as we strolled as nonchalantly as we could away from the barracks. We crossed a railway and came to a wide tarmac road which we followed for a short distance until a large German staff car swept past. Then we rather lost our nerve and took to the fields again. At one point we pushed our way through a thick hedge to be confronted by a deep stream about ten feet wide. We tried to swing across this on overhanging branches but the attempt proved a dismal failure. We both fell in and were soaked from head to foot. Worse, the biscuits which we had saved as the mainstay of our diet also suffered so we had to eat them there and then before they disintegrated completely. Then we continued on our way, water squelching out of our boots and looking more like frogmen than the two Belgian peasants we were supposed to be. All the time we were worrying about Fred and Peter and hoping that they had managed to get clear. It was not until after the war that I learnt the sad news that they had been recaptured.

Our plan was to make our way by whatever means presented itself and, if necessary, entirely on foot to Free

France in the hope that from there we would be able to find a boat or escape through Spain. Accordingly we set a south-westerly course and, being unable to make a more detailed plan, having no map, we just hoped for the best.

It was obvious that we could not escape from Belgium without relying to some extent on the Belgians so, when we saw a solitary labourer working amongst some roots, we decided that the sooner we tested the rumours we had heard about Belgian disloyalty the better. He was an elderly man and at once guessed what we were. With luck we might have fooled a particularly dumb German but with the local population we had no chance whatsoever.

To our immense relief he proved to be kindness itself. He at once took us to his cottage which he shared with an elderly sister and gave us a good meal. Then he stocked us up with eggs, bread and butter and—a gift from the Gods —the most excellent road map which took us up to the Franco-Belgian frontier and well into France. It was an even better map than Peter's so we had won hands down over the compass deal.

We were still frightened that when our escape was discovered there would be a hue and cry so we pressed on with all speed in an effort to get over the frontier, which was six or seven miles away. The elements were, however, against us. At about midday it came on to rain which soon developed into a downpour. Our boots became so clogged with mud that we could scarcely lift one foot after the other. As the frontier was not far we sheltered in a shed, sharing it with a number of cows and their calves. We were so closely packed together that it was difficult to avoid a further deterioration in our appearance when they answered the calls of nature, which seemed to be unnaturally often. We were very glad when the skies cleared and we were able to push on.

Now that we had food for our immediate needs we were keen to avoid the increasing number of people we came across working in the fields—mostly children and old people—so it necessitated making a number of tiresome detours but none the less we made good progress. In the middle of the afternoon we topped a small rise and found ourselves looking down on a barbed wire entanglement and beyond a row of pillboxes. *La belle France* was once more before us.

The crossing presented no difficulties. It was rather pathetic to think that this was the line manned so diligently by the B.E.F. all the winter and spring. Now the defences stood abandoned without a bullet mark showing on any of the pillboxes. After all that effort they had been given up without a struggle.

We decided to head for a small hamlet called Pont Thibault. To get there we had to cross two main roads, which we did with some trepidation, but no one paid us any attention and we went on our way confidently. When we came to an absolutely straight pavé road lined with poplar trees heading in the direction we wanted to go we thankfully abandoned the fields and followed it for some miles. Now that our clothes were dried out we would escape notice from any passing German vehicle. Johnnie was wearing an old coat and some worsted trousers while I had a suit of dungarees and we both had little blue berets. We did not trust our disguise sufficiently, however, to risk walking through a populated area, so when we came to a little village we took to the fields again.

All went well until we came to a large corrugated barn and, rounding a corner, practically walked into the arms of a man forking hay from a cart. He looked at us curiously but simply smiled and went on with his work. Clearly we had not deceived him but he had decided to take no notice.

We had walked for almost twelve hours and must have covered, with detours, about twenty miles when we at last came to the outskirts of Pont Thibault. Johnnie had been billeted there a few months earlier and had made several friends. We were now to test their loyalty.

The first house we visited belonged to an elderly wine merchant called Monsieur Vaubeck and he was sitting having his evening meal with his wife when we walked in. For a few long seconds they gazed at us as if we were ghosts; then the woman let out a cry "C'est Blondé!" and a moment later we were all shaking hands and embracing. Poor Johnnie did not have the ideal appearance for an escaper. I looked British enough but Johnnie with his golden hair and pink complexion could never possibly be mistaken for a Frenchman. During the whole time we were to stay in the district he was universally known as "Blondé".

Within an hour of our arrival the whole of the village seemed to know about us. While we tucked into an enormous meal of omelettes and steaks, they came into the house, sometimes six at a time, to greet us. Of course it was bad security but with so much friendliness from such honest simple folk, what could we do but accept the situation?

It was such a night of rejoicing and festivity that it was almost midnight before we were sent to the Vaubeck's own feather bed whilst they made do in chairs. We fell instantly asleep, feeling secure and happy after eighteen hours of continual strain and tension.

Pont Thibault is a small hamlet some six miles to the south-west of Lille on the main Lille–Douai road. Workmen's cottages line the road while a pavé side road forming the stem of a "T" leads off in the centre, also lined on each side by cottages. It is the centre of a farming community in which all farmers, however small, own their own land

and, although some owned larger acreages than others, there was general social equality. As with all the farming communities in France at that time there was an acute shortage of labour, most young men having been taken prisoner or directed into some kind of labour force.

It was soon made clear to us that we would be welcome to live amongst them if we would lend a hand in the fields. The harvest was approaching and even two extra labourers in the work squad could make quite a difference. During the harvest in particular work was done on a co-operative basis, several farmers banding together to help each other. It was an arrangement with which we were only too happy to fall in as it gave us some time to make proper plans as well as gather such equipment as we should need for continuing our travels.

The first problem was to find somewhere permanent to stay and it was decided that we should split up, as the two of us together would be too much of a burden on a single family. However, we must be close enough so that we could meet to plan together in the evenings.

There was one farm larger than the rest known as the "Stork Farm" after the life-sized models of two storks and their family perched on the roof. It was the home of a well-to-do family who had fled before the advancing Germans to their villa in the South of France. They had left a woman called Rosa in charge, helped by her younger brother Paul. Paul was one of the few men of military age in the village and I at first wondered why he had not been called up like the rest. When I got to know him better I realized that he was abnormal and must have failed his medical test. In fact the whole family, including the mother who lived with them, were considered slightly mad by the rest of the village. None the less it was decided that this should be my quarters on the grounds that they were best able to afford to keep me. To give them their due they installed me in the best bedroom. It had beautiful furniture and a majestic four-poster bed into which I rolled contentedly each night.

Johnnie's accommodation was more modest. He was put at a small farm on the main road about five hundred yards from Stork Farm. It was run by a woman called Alice who was the youngest of four sisters three of whom were married to local farmers. The second sister was a Madame Maille whose husband we learnt was the man who had smiled at us when we came upon him forking hay. The Maille farm was on the fringe of Ennevelin, a village about a mile from Pont Thibault. The eldest sister, a Madame Depuis, lived nearer Lille, equidistant from Madame Maille and Alice.

The arrangement was that one night we would both eat at Stork Farm and the next night at Alice's and this worked admirably. On the whole, in spite of my more luxurious surroundings, it was Johnnie who had the best of the bargain. Alice was full of fun and accepted the situation completely. Rosa, Paul and their mother on the other hand were slightly hostile. I was compensated, however, by two men who worked at Stork Farm, Francois and Louis. Each was old enough to be my grandfather but they were immensely kind to me. Francois in particular took me under his wing and treated me as his own son.

Unlike Johnnie, I had not been brought up in the country and found the farm work both arduous and difficult. Before the harvest started Francois used to put me to the comparatively easy task of cleaning the farm implements and machinery and gave me the minimum of the back breaking work of hoeing roots. I caused great amusement when I said that I was "*nettoyant les chariots*".

Alice fed us like fighting cocks. Great lumps of very tender steak with piles of *pommes frites*, as only the French can cook them, masses of fresh white bread and butter with

11 Sally Siauve Evausy in Red Cross uniform outside her house in Rue Solferino, Lille.

12 Sally with Siegfried, the great dane.

13 Georges Siauve Evausy, Sally's flamboyant husband.

home-made fruit compotes, more tasty than jam, was the staple meal and woe betide us if we left anything on our plates. Alice insisted that we wipe them clean before we could claim to be finished and soon we were putting on weight in spite of the exercise of our farming activities.

From Alice's house by the roadside we could watch the German transport roll past every day. This familiarity with the sight of the enemy without there being any immediate chance of our being detected gave us a false sense of confidence and we would have grown careless if it had not been for the occasional rude reminder of our vulnerability. One day, for example, I was having my lunch in a back room at Stork Farm when a German Air Force Captain paid an informal visit. He was friendly enough but Rosa, whose nerves were not very good at the best of times, was considerably shaken and I began to feel that it would be wiser if I were to move elsewhere.

A few days later Johnnie had a worse experience. Five of them, including Johnnie, were sitting having a meal when a German officer walked into the room without any warning. Johnnie had his back to the door but from the looks of consternation on the faces of the others, he knew it was an unwanted intruder. He continued to stare straight ahead not daring to turn round for fear that his very British looks should give him away. It was only another German wanting milk and eggs but the contact was too close to be comfortable.

We had not been at Pont Thibault long before considerable excitement was caused by the arrival of the brother of the absent owner of Stork Farm. He was also an escapee and was trying to reach France Libre to join his relations. He apparently also did not trust Rosa and her family and indeed stayed in the next village for fear that somebody might give him away. He was a good chap and we spent

81

many hours together discussing various methods of escape. His plan was simplicity itself—to get on to a bicycle and keep riding. He was quite willing that we should go with him, but Johnnie and I decided against it. We were not prepared to take such a plunge at that moment. I did hear later that some British soldiers had in fact cycled success-fully out of Occupied France.

It was becoming increasingly obvious to me that Stork Farm was far from an ideal refuge. I felt that Paul in particular was not to be trusted and Rosa was too easily thrown into a panic. One day I was working in the fields as usual when Paul came rushing out to the field, waving his hands and shouting, "Les Boches! Les Boches!" at the top of his voice. I made a desperate sprint for cover in a corn-field and lay for a long time hardly daring to move until I discovered that it was just some figment of his fevered brain or perhaps just a device to get rid of me.

It was after this incident that I started actively to make arrangements to move elsewhere and, as a result of discus sions with Alice, it was decided that I should go and live at the Maille's Farm.

Madame Maille was one of the most remarkable of many remarkable people I was to meet in the next few months She was much less volatile than her sister Alice but had a quiet dignity which was most impressive. She was a "good" woman in every sense of the word. Deeply religious she carried her beliefs into her everyday life. I never heard her being unkind about anyone and her generosity to me was something I shall never forget. Both she and her husband, François, had the courage of lions. François Maille was rather rougher-hewn with a more obvious sense of humour, a liking for his beer and wine and a general bonhomie, but he was also a devout man and as straightforward as you could wish. They had two sons, François and Michel, who were still under military age and helped on the farm.

After Stork Farm, life in the Maille household was very much more pleasant and we soon fell into a comfortable routine. My name, Derek, did not fit in very well with the French language so I was re-christened Pierre—or rather Grand Pierre to distinguish me from Alice's eight-year-old son who became Petit Pierre. Johnnie became naturally Jean when he wasn't Blondé and we kept these names during the whole of our stay in France.

Our days were spent out in the fields and most nights when Petit Pierre came home from school, Johnnie and I would play football with him. He hated to be beaten so we would take care to kick the ball to him gently so as not to cause an outburst of tears. After the experiences we had been through it would have been an idyllic existence if it had not been for the continual reminders that we were fugitives.

Another such reminder occurred soon after I moved to the Mailles. I was talking to Madame in the parlour one day when we heard the tramp of boots outside. She went to the window and peered into the yard, then signalled to me urgently with her hands behind her back to make myself scarce. I slipped into the pantry and closed the door just in time. A moment later a German soldier walked in and started questioning her. It appeared that he was one of a party searching the village for British arms and uniform. Madame Maille answered him calmly and quietly and then handing him a British army groundsheet which hung behind the parlour door, told him it was all she had. He was so pleased to make a "find" that he went away quite happily. I was much more shaken by the incident than she was and yet she was undoubtedly in the greater danger if I had undoubtedly been caught.

Work at the Maille farm was quite hard going. We went to the fields early in the morning and only returned for a late mid-day meal. Then we worked on again until supper time. Looking back now I laugh at myself for my ineptitude at farm work. One of our more tiresome chores as the harvest approached was cutting out the weeds from amongst the corn. The others were of course expert but I invariably finished with almost as much corn as weeds. The Mailles often sang while they worked and their songs were usually an expression of what they thought of their German conquerors. Often they referred to them as "*Les Doriphores*", which was a term which puzzled me until I learned with some amusement that it was the local name given to a particularly nasty insect that eats the potato crop and was the scourge of farms in the area.

The Mailles, like all their neighbours, were Catholics and much was made of Sunday. I would have been quite content to go about in my workaday clothes but they would have none of it. I must dress up like the rest of them and for this purpose I was presented with an old but very passable brown lounge suit. The only thing they could not get me to do was to wear the ludicrous hat which they tried to wish upon me. Of course it would have been most unwise for me to go to the church so I spent most of Sunday lying out in the sun in my fine suit reading a collection of English paperback books which the villagers had brought me.

It was about a week after I had moved to the Mailles that I met the village school mistress, Lucille. She was attractive and likeable, very intelligent, but also highly strung and at times intense. The war had brought her a great sadness. Her brother was missing and she did not know if he was dead or alive and her husband was a prisoner in a town about twenty miles away where she seldom got to see him. As she spoke good English she undertook to help me improve my French. I was required to sit down to my homework each evening like any schoolboy and I managed to make quite good progress.

It was through Lucille that I first met the local pig merchant. He was a big fat man, talkative to the point of garrulousness and with great open-handed generosity. One of the first things he asked when we met was how I was off for money. When I confessed that I had none he immediately opened his wallet and presented me with five hundred francs, between three and four pounds. Although I was to meet him again after the war he would never let me repay the loan.

Lucille's object in introducing him to me was to assist our escape plan. He was a man with wide contacts and one of the very few people allowed to run a van in which he delivered pork to customers for many miles around. When we were shown into his house, he seated himself behind his desk, folded his hands in front of him and peered at me with benevolent interest—for all the world like a solicitor preparing to advise a client.

His first suggestion was that he should make contact with some escape organization of which he knew in Lille. When he had done this we met again and he told me that he had the names of some people who could prepare false papers and identity cards and that he could guarantee their good faith. This sounded to me like a big step forward but Lucille was not so convinced. She thought we should check their bona fides from another quarter. At this the pig merchant took offence, considering that his word as "an honourable Frenchman" was good enough. Quite an argument developed between them with me putting in a word here and there to try and keep the peace but in the end nothing definite was decided. The pig merchant did, however, offer me a lift in his van if ever I wanted to go anywhere. "Concealed under my pigs, Monsieur, you will be quite safe." It was an offer I hoped I should not have to take up.

Now the harvest was starting and every spare hand was needed in the fields. The cutting round the sides of each field was done by scythe and the sheaves bound by hand. I was absolutely hopeless at binding, the twisting of the knot always defeating me so that it took me as long to tie one as even the youngest Maille boy took to do four. None the less I struggled on as best I could but all the time I was thinking that soon the harvest would be over and we would be outstaying our welcome. We had already imposed ourselves on these excellent people for almost a month and it was becoming urgent that we should move on.

One Sunday the Mailles decided that it was time I was introduced to the eldest sister, Madame Depuis, whose husband's farm was a couple of miles away. Accordingly Monsieur Maille and I set off after lunch to walk there across the fields. Our welcome was warm enough but there was a certain reserve until my genuineness was established, whereupon Madame Depuis showed herself to be as warm-hearted as her two sisters. After about an hour we were joined by her husband and their buxom seventeen-year-old daughter Marguerite, who had been out for a walk. Monsieur Depuis enquired closely who I was. He then went out and came back with two young men whom I took to be his sons. My surprise was, therefore, considerable when I shook hands with them to be greeted with two very English "How do you do's". They were two young private soldiers of the Lothian and Border Horse called Arthur and Daniel. I never discovered their surnames. Arthur was nineteen and Daniel only just eighteen, having faked his age in order to join up. The security in the Depuis household was so good that they had lived there rather longer than we had been in the district and we had never heard even a rumour of their presence. Monsieur Depuis looked after them as if they were his own children. I think he would have given his life for them and when the time came for us British to leave the district it was very hard to persuade him to let them go.

The three of us had a great time swopping stories of our experiences. They showed me their room with great pride, again the best in the house, and pressed me to share their store of cigarettes and books. They were desperately nervous and hardly dared to leave the vicinity of the house. For two boys of their age to be hunted for their lives was indeed a nerve-racking experience.

We returned to the Maille farm late that evening to be greeted with the news that the village had been combed by a German agent searching for British soldiers. He had asked Madame Maille many questions and we all felt that somebody in the village must have been too talkative. It was alarming news and made me all the more determined that we must get away soon. I had not seen anything of Johnnie since the harvest had started but it was obvious that we must get together so I sent a message by Petit Pierre on his way home from school that I would be over for lunch the following Sunday.

In fact I could have saved myself the trouble for the following day Johnnie arrived and, to my astonishment, he had two very pretty girls, Yvonne and Hélène, with him. Yvonne was his old girlfriend whom he had asked about through the railings when we were imprisoned in Kléber Barracks. He had sent her a letter and she had cycled out straight away with her friend to meet us, such was the magnetic power "Blondé" had with the girls.

They were anxious to get back to Pont Thibault so that within a few minutes Johnnie and I were cycling down the

pavé road with a girl each on the handlebars of their bicycles. Of course it was sheer madness but it all happened
so suddenly and they were such attractive creatures that
we got quite carried away!

The risks we took did not end with the bicycle ride. Back
at Alice's house we gathered in the front room, which was
right along the roadside, and they chattered away in English
at the top of their voices. They even sang English songs, one
of their favourites being "Oh Johnnie! Oh, Johnnie!
How you can love", which sent them into peals of laughter.
Then they taught us "Daisy Bell" in French and I can still
remember the last line "On a bicycle made for two" which
was rendered as *"Dans petit tandem tous les deux!"* They
were a most happy-go-lucky couple and after they had gone
I felt ashamed that I had been so fussy about their keeping
their voices down, but as there was a broken window-pane
in the parlour which allowed everything to be heard clearly
in the street perhaps I was justified.

They promised to come back in a fortnight but whether
they did or not I shall never know because by then we
had gone.

After the girls had left I made my way, as I had already
arranged, to have tea with the Depuis family. When I
arrived it was to find that there was a couple already there
—a middle-aged lady and her daughter. They turned out to
be representatives from an escape organization in Lille and
they had heard through a network operated from the little
cafe opposite the Mailles' farm that we were in the neighbourhood. They had walked from the city to contact us
and had brought with them some additional clothing
including, much to my joy, a splendid pair of brown walking shoes which fitted me perfectly. They had come over
purely to find out how matters stood so that they could
alert their friends in Lille. There was nothing to be done

at the moment but to go back to the harvesting and await developments, but I was very encouraged.

Developments were not long in coming. In the second week in August I received an urgent message to go to the Depuis' farm as soon as possible as there was some good news for me. Almost sick with excitement, I set off straight away across the fields. This time I was ushered into the presence of a man and woman who came from Lille and who claimed that they had been sent by the head of the escape organization which operated under cover of the Croix Rouge. We talked for about an hour while I tried to make up my mind if they were to be trusted. Lucille had made me suspicious of accepting anyone at face value for she claimed that there were quite a few people dabbling in helping escapers who were not reliable.

When my new acquaintances left it was with the general understanding that we should, all four, move shortly into hiding in Lille from where it would be easier to make further plans.

I would not have been altogether happy about this had not yet another woman arrived a couple of days later when I was again summoned to the Depuis farm. This time I took Lucille with me as I considered she was a better judge of her own compatriots than I was. However, I had no doubt about the woman we met this time. She was well dressed, in her thirties and spoke English well. She was quite obviously a person of standing and influence. She explained that she was the head of the organization which had sent the other two and that she had come to make final plans for our departure. At one stage she took Lucille into another room and I could overhear a considerable argument taking place. When Lucille emerged she was in floods of tears but it was not until after the lady had gone that I got the story of what had upset her. Apparently she had admitted that she had been trying to help us by asking the advice of several acquaintances but instead of getting a pat on the back she had been soundly taken to task for talking too much.

Our new friend told us in no uncertain terms that the security had been so bad and so many people knew about us that we must leave as soon as possible. As she drove away we saw that she had a large Red Cross painted on the back window of her car and we felt that we had at last fallen into the right hands.

It was on the morning of 12 August that I got a message to report to the Depuis farm with all my belongings. It could only mean one thing, so I bid Madame Maille a tearful farewell. Her husband and the boys were out in the fields so leaving warm messages of affection for them I left the farm for the last time.

At the Depuis' I found that the first man to visit us was there, having cycled out from Lille, bringing with him a second machine. I was to go first and Johnnie was to follow in a few days. My guide's name was Robert.

Without more ado we set off side by side riding our bicycles down the pavé road into a new world. Strangely, the surroundings I was leaving seemed very secure and the future filled me with dread.

Chapter 5

I did not enjoy the journey to Lille. Shortly after we had turned right into the main Douai–Lille road we had to pass the aerodrome. It was covered with heavily camouflaged twin-engined bombers which I noted were strictly guarded —two sentries to each plane. My guide, whose name was Robert, told me that French patriots had been stealing up to two planes a week until the guards had been doubled. One French pilot had pinched a Messerschmitt 109 which happened to be on the airfield with the bombers and had had the nerve to machine-gun the hangars before setting off across the Channel for England.

A few miles past the aerodrome we came to the outskirts of Lille and there were many Germans strolling along the pavements. I was seized with a ridiculous fear that I might fall off or do something equally silly and so attract attention to myself. To increase my agony we had to stop for some five minutes at a level crossing, surrounded by stationary cars and other cyclists. I felt quite sure that somebody would speak to us and that the game would be up, but everything passed off without incident.

We did not, much to my relief, have to pass through the centre of the town. Instead we turned off down a side street of slum houses which ended in a cul-de-sac. Entering a grimy looking building, we climbed four flights of dark, rickety stairs to a small apartment where we were greeted by Robert's wife, Marie, who turned out to be the woman I had already met at the Depuis'. She was much more communicative than her husband and gave me a motherly welcome. She also told me of her work for the Croix Rouge and showed me her uniform as proof of her identity. She was full of praise for the lady who had come out to see us and make the arrangements for the first step of our journey to freedom. There were still a large number of British wounded in German-controlled French hospitals and her work as a senior member of the Red Cross provided a valuable cover.

In spite of the warmth of my welcome, however, I felt very uneasy. This did not spring from any doubts about the loyalty of Robert and Marie but because they were obviously extremely poor and my presence must have been a heavy drain on their slim resources. On that first day they pressed a huge dish of steak and onions on me which I felt sure they could ill afford. Also, after the freedom of my life on the farm, I felt I should go mad if I had to live for very long in this tiny two-roomed flat.

My worries were short-lived. In the middle of the after-noon following my arrival, Marie rushed in to say that her chief had arrived to take me away. A moment later I was being ushered into a waiting motor car and given a Red Cross armband to slip over my sleeve. I did not much like the idea of masquerading as a Red Cross official as I could imagine the trouble it would cause if I were discovered, but they insisted.

There followed a drive into the centre of the town, along the boulevards crowded with Germans, until we finally stopped in a smart street, the Rue Solferino, by large studded double doors. The car's horn was sounded, the doors swung open and we drove into a spacious courtyard. As we got out of the car a huge Great Dane, answering to the name of Siegfried, nearly knocked us over with his excited welcome.

At last came the time for introductions. My saviour's name was Sally Siauve Evausy and she was married to a well-known surgeon called Georges of whom we were later to see a great deal. The house was a splendid mansion with fine big rooms and a view over the main street where one could sit and look out behind lace curtains without fear of being seen. I was disappointed to learn that this was not to be my new home and that I had another journey to make, this time on foot with Sally's nephew, Jean, as my guide. To tell the truth I had been a little bit intimidated by Sally at first but after an hour of general conversation, I realized what a human person she was and that her front of cool efficiency covered a very warm-hearted personality.

The journey we now had to make on foot only took a matter of ten minutes but I found it agonizing. Jean kept up a loud one-sided conversation to which I replied in monosyllables while I was on the look-out all the time for suspicious stares from the passers-by. Our destination turned out to be a block of flats and my new home was in the top one up four flights of stairs.

When Jean rang the bell the door was opened just a crack by an elderly lady. A whispered conversation followed, the door opened a little wider and we both slipped inside.

To my surprise the little room we now entered was filled with people. There were four girls and two small boys and they were joined immediately by a dear old man with a beard who came in from another room. When the girls learned that I was a Captain in the British Army, it was as if the Prince of Wales himself had dropped in for a visit. They all rushed about laying the table for a meal and the girls, who all knew a little English, pushed each other aside in an effort to try out their knowledge on me. My French was still deplorable and their English little better but after a time with the help of sign language we got on famously.

Now I was in for another surprise. I learned that there were already two English soldiers concealed in the flat. They lived upstairs in the attic but the occasion was considered to be such an important one that it was decided that it was worth the risk of bringing them down to introduce me.

Edward and Charlie were two privates in the Lincolnshire Regiment who had never been captured but had lived off the land ever since the fall of Dunkirk. We shook hands vigorously, feeling rather like Stanley meeting two Livingstones. They had been holed up in a farm where Sally had found them and brought them into Lille.

It took a little time to sort out just who everybody was. The family consisted of three daughters; Suzanne, aged twenty-two, Marguerite, aged nineteen, and Françoise, aged seventeen, and the young boy Jean, a rather precocious eleven. The girls were all most attractive—particularly Suzanne and Françoise—and friendly almost to the point of embarrassment. The fourth girl was a school friend of Françoise's and the second small boy a friend of Jean's. We were worried about such a young boy knowing of our presence and were afraid that he might give us away by idle chatter with his friends. However, he turned out to be very security conscious and paid us a number of calls, never failing to bring us a packet of cigarettes from his parents' apparently unending store.

After tea Charlie and Edward took me up to the attic to see our quarters. They consisted of a small single room equipped with a double bed for the boys and a camp bed for me. There was also a bare six-foot table round which

94

we took our meals, sitting on the bed at one side and pack-
ing cases on the other.

I was a bit taken aback at the smallness of the room but
I was hardly in a position to complain. When, two days
later, Johnnie arrived to join us, the overcrowding was
made worse. He had to sleep on some cushions on the floor.
That was not, however, the end of it. A few days later
Arthur and Daniel appeared and were given an old mattress
which took up the whole of the rest of the floor space.

Apparently there had been quite a scene when Sally had
arrived to take the two boys away from the Depuis'. Both
boys had burst into tears at the prospect of leaving the
farm. So too had Madame Depuis, who wanted to keep
them for the rest of the war. There had been almost a
stand-up fight but Sally had got her way. She only persuaded
them that it was the best course by making the threat that
the officers (Johnnie and me) would take action if they refused. The poor lads were so frightened of undertaking the
journey that they had to be taken all the way by car instead
of cycling and for the first few days in the attic they
were in despair.

The rest of us got on quite well together. Edward and
Charlie had a rudimentary knowledge of whist while
Johnnie and I had an even rougher idea of the rules of
contract. Undeterred we set ourselves the task of learning
bridge and spent many happy hours playing a game which
amused us but would have made the experts weep.

During the phoney war each of the three daughters had
found a boy friend amongst the British troops stationed in
Lille. We were shown photographs of them and asked to
judge which was the best looking and when, amidst much
teasing and laughter, we gave our vote, the two losers were
quite downcast. There was great excitement when it was
discovered that Suzanne's boy friend was in hospital in

Lille and immediately plans were made for his escape. I never knew if anything came of them.

I do not know how our generous hosts managed to feed us all but somehow they managed to give us ample meals —I suspect by going short themselves. Sally helped by bringing food from her house and possibly gave them some money but we never learned the exact details. Before our arrival Charlie and Edward had been accustomed to go walking with the girls in the afternoon but we soon put a stop to this. However cramped our quarters were it was not worth the risk of spending the rest of the war in a prison camp for the sake of a little exercise.

After that the family used to visit us at some time each day and we would tell each other stories in French and English which helped to pass the time. Sally came every other day, usually just before dark. She had many other escapees hiding in other parts of the town but I think we were her favourites. One evening she brought with her a Red Cross nurse who seemed to know more about details of the next stage of our escape than Sally. We questioned her closely but she would give little away, just allowing us to know enough to realize that something was being done so as to keep up our morale.

Jean, Sally's nephew, who also visited us, was more forthcoming. He told us of a plan to signal to England on a short wave radio for a plane to be sent over which would land on the flat fields after the harvest had been brought in. A group of us was to be assembled on that occasion at a central point somewhere in the country and lifted out to safety. He told us that this had been accomplished several times and even gave us details of one escapee who had panicked at the last moment and had to be knocked out before he could be taken aboard. However fantastic all this may now seem, we were quite prepared to believe anything and listened with excitement to every word we were told.

Another visitor was the old farmer who had harboured Charlie and Edward before they came to Lille and who brought us welcome supplies of eggs and butter. He, too, had a scheme for our escape. He told us that there was a boatman in Cherbourg who rowed escapees across the Channel two or three times a week and that he knew the address of the people who could put us in contact with him. We discussed it eagerly but this plan also came to nothing.

There was one rather alarming occasion when Françoise brought a tall, dark boy dressed in a lounge suit and beret to our hideaway. We took him to be French and were worried at another outsider knowing our whereabouts. It turned out that he too was English and he told us at length how he spent his time wandering into cafes in Lille and striking up conversations with the French. He even boasted of having a German as a friend who claimed to be anti-Nazi and with whom he had long conversations. All this infuriated me. Although his disguise was excellent his French was appalling and I felt that he was running quite unnecessary risks which not only endangered himself but all those gallant people who were helping him. If he could move about so freely, it was surely better that he made some attempt to get out of France instead of hanging around to everyone's peril. I sternly forbade him ever to visit us again.

Although our imprisonment in the attic was extremely irksome, the kindness of our hosts made up for a great deal. While we were living there Johnnie had his twenty-second birthday and Sally was determined that it should be properly celebrated. On the day we were all invited down to the flat where, to our surprise, there was a table spread out with many delicacies and in the centre a huge

97

cake with twenty-two candles on it. We had a great party, fourteen of us sitting down together. Afterwards Françoise played a selection of French and English songs which we sang as softly as possible as the walls of the apartment were very thin. We did not return upstairs until very late that night but thoroughly refreshed by such a pleasant break.

On another day, Sally arrived with four brand new suits for me to try on which she had got from the tailor on the pretext that they were for her husband. She said that she could not bear looking at my old suit any longer and insisted that I choose one. I got one that really fitted me well and it was to last me until the end of my travels.

There was a wireless in the flat and the family used to listen to the B.B.C. regularly and report the news to us. In this way we learnt of the Battle of Britain and felt thoroughly impotent as we heard of the bombing of our cities. Even more dramatic than the reported news was the evidence of our own eyes. Frequently huge formations of German bombers would fly overhead so low that they seemed to skim the roof tops and the noise was deafening. If the idea was to impress the population with their might it had the opposite effect for some hours later the bombers would return and it was obvious to everyone that they had suffered heavy losses. Everybody listened to the British bulletins as well as the heavily censored German versions and morale was given a great boost when they realized that the British reports of heavy German losses were accurate.

Occasionally there were other snippets of news to excite us. We heard that there had been several attempts to invade Britain but that all of them had failed for one reason or another. We also heard that Germans had been seen being marched through the streets of Lille in irons for refusing to fly sorties over Britain and that sometimes pilots had to be forced into their planes at pistol point.

One of the perils of our day-to-day existence was the presence of two old women who acted as caretakers in the building. The family were certain that they would give us away if they ever discovered our presence and while they went about the job of sweeping the stairs we kept as quiet as mice.

After ten days in the attic, however, we had gradually become less security-conscious. The girls spent longer and longer each day talking and laughing with us and were not so careful about their comings and goings. One night we really thought we had given the game away. There were shots in the road below and we were sure that the Germans had discovered our hideaway. It turned out that we had left our light on with the windows open and the shots were a warning to observe the black-out. It was an extraordinarily stupid thing to have done.

Two days after this incident something more serious happened and again it was due to our carelessness. Somehow we had left our door unlocked and in the middle of the morning a completely strange woman walked in. She looked at us in amazement for a moment and quickly disappeared. When Mama and the girls came up with our midday meal we told them what had happened. Immediately Mama burst into hysterical tears. The concierge she might have been able to deal with but to be discovered by one of the neighbours was dreadful.

When Sally came that evening we held a council of war and it was decided that it was too dangerous for us to stay any longer but the problem of where to move us to was a difficult one. Sally decided that it was too much to ask one loyal family to harbour six Britishers and we would have to be split up.

Next morning Johnnie and I received a message that we were to be ready to move that night. Sally herself called for us and we bade our fond farewells to the family and our comrades. We never saw them again. We learnt that we were going to Sally's own house and followed her obediently down the street, hurrying as Frenchmen would, caught out after curfew time. We only passed a few other civilians and two Germans who took no notice of us. In ten minutes we were safely behind the great studded doors.

We went up to Sally's bedroom and at once turned on the radio. When we got London to my great delight it was to hear Archie MacNab of the Glasgow Police playing the bagpipes. Almost exactly a year earlier I had heard him play at the South Uist Games where I was on a recruiting campaign. I was so excited that to Sally's complete astonishment and amusement I leaped to my feet and started to dance a vigorous Highland Fling.

We were now to have the privilege of staying permanently with Sally and she immediately set about throwing everyone off our trail. Anyone who knew that she had been helping us was now told that we had moved on and that she had no idea where we were hiding. As additional security she would not even tell us what arrangements had been made for our late companions.

That night Johnnie slept in the room which was to be his for the rest of our stay but, my room not yet being ready, I was put in the surgery. In this way I was the first to meet Sally's husband, the redoubtable Georges. I awoke to find Sally standing beside my bed with this splendid looking man in the uniform of a French Officer.

Georges plays an important part in my narrative so I will introduce him properly. He was a man of many parts. All over the house there were pictures of him in his bathing trunks showing off his fine physique, for in his youth he had been a champion weight lifter—a sport which is as popular in France as boxing is in England. At the same time he was a man of great intellectual attainments. He was a brilliant classicist and well-read in the philosophies and he was a leader in his chosen profession as a surgeon.

Above all Georges was a patriot. He had a passionate love of his country and the presence of the Germans affected him like an illness. In the first war he had been mentioned in dispatches and awarded the Croix de Guerre and in this war he had commanded a Field Ambulance Unit until France was overrun. He had been working as a surgeon at the hospital at St Omer under the supervision of the Germans and being over the age of call up was allowed to move about more freely providing he reported to the local Kommandateur once a week. However he found this situation intolerable and so had resigned and come back to live at home. Every morning he would ride out of Lille on his powerful motorbike to get fresh air into his lungs and the stink of the Germans out of his nostrils.

His greatest ambition was to escape from France and join de Gaulle in London. He would pace up and down the drawing-room carpet for hours delivering a tirade against the Germans and all their works. He had spells of being boastful and bombastic but he had a redeeming sense of humour and he was to prove a courageous companion and a staunch friend.

For us the house was a wonderful change after our cramped quarters in the attic. It was a large place with three stories and four rooms on each floor. Johnnie and I had a room each on the top floor where Sally's young niece, Anne Marie, also had a room. There were two rooms on the ground floor at the back of the house which opened into one another to make one big room. Here we spent most of our time, eating at one end and using the other end to sit. It looked out on to the yard, approximately forty-five feet by fifteen, which was surrounded by a high wall so that it was not overlooked. We used the yard a lot after dark to get fresh air and a little exercise. For the rest we did physical jerks in the dining-room to try and keep ourselves fit.

It was not long before the days started to fall into a pattern. We came down for lunch and dinner to the ground floor and spent the time in between listening to the wireless, reading or playing cards. After dinner, Sally would play the piano for us, which she did quite beautifully. Most of the time she would play the classics. She had to be careful when she played Chopin as, being of Polish birth, his music was banned by the Germans—an example of their extraordinary narrow-mindedness. When she came to the end of an evening recital she would always play "God Save the King" followed by the "Marseillaise".

This routine, pleasant enough though it was, was not good for our health. The boredom sapped our energy so that the slightest thing seemed too much of an effort. We soon shrank from the thought of our next step to freedom and were fearful of the future. To pass the time we smoked far too much. Georges—whom we always called "Le Commandant" out of respect for his years—was a heavy smoker with a great selection of pipes which he insisted we used as we wanted. There was a cherrywood of which I was particularly fond, with a long curly stem so that I could rest the bowl on my chest and puff away contentedly all afternoon. Whatever else was in short supply in France it was certainly not tobacco. Georges had bowls and bowls of it. Of course we were lucky to live with a well-off family and did not feel the food shortages in the same way that the poorer families were already beginning to.

There was one other member of the household whom I have not so far mentioned. This was Georges' little Moroccan servant who had been with him for years and accompanied him wherever he went. Always known as "Maroc" he took a great liking for Johnnie and me and would do anything for us. Like his master he considered the British to be the saviours of Europe and longed for the day when he could get back to his home in Casablanca and carry on the fight. Whenever he went shopping he used to return in tears, for the Germans used to insult him and even kick him in the street.

Knowing the marked danger of this enforced inactivity we were impatient for any news of a possible escape route. Georges was intensely jealous of Sally having active work to do every day while he had nothing to occupy him. It made him irritable and sometimes he would thump the table angrily declaring, "Secret matters are bound to go wrong when handled by women!" Just the same, whenever Sally came in at night, we would all three rush to her and demand the latest news. Usually her reply was, "Patience, patience!" but patience was something none of us had much of.

There was great excitement when Sally returned to the house one evening and, pulling up her skirt, took a folded paper from the top of her stocking. It was an exact map of the gun positions at Cap Gris Nez from which the Channel and Dover itself were regularly shelled. We now realized that Sally had other fish to fry besides assisting escaping prisoners. She regularly sent reports to England of troop movements and positions via agents by short wave radio. She knew of no less than eleven secret stations operating around Lille and of a twelfth which was discovered by the Germans but from where the operator had fortunately escaped. Although it was still early days it was remarkable how the resistance organization was building up. It had not of course yet reached the level of intense activity it was later to achieve, but it already occupied practically the whole of Sally's time.

German morale was suffering badly as the appointed date

for the invasion came and went. The air raids, too, did not seem to be having the expected effect and reports of heavy casualties amongst the German planes cheered us greatly. It was while we were with Georges and Sally that Hitler paid a visit to Lille, accompanied by Goering. This was a disappointment as we had heard a rumour that Goering was dead, machine-gunned by a single British plane near Le Havre where supposedly he had been to organize a new invasion. However grotesque were the rumours we were only too keen to believe them.

Lille had been under German occupation during most of the 1914–18 war and the inhabitants were experienced at underground resistance, which they put to good account in 1940. Underground activity was rife and the occupying troops had much trouble trying to suppress it. In 1916 there had been four leading resisters all of whom were caught and shot. After the war a marble sculpture had been built as a memorial to them in one of the main streets. It showed three of the men blindfolded awaiting the firing squad while a fourth lay dead at their feet. One day the Germans blew up this memorial. The infuriated townsfolk retaliated by desecrating a German cemetery, pulling up the crosses and despoiling the graves. It was not a very intelligent act of revenge but showed the depth of their feelings. The Germans retaliated in their turn by imposing a huge fine on the city and tightening up on all security measures. The courage of the people of Lille was remarkable. It was estimated that the number of British concealed by townsfolk at this time ran into four figures.

The penalties threatened against the civilian population were severe and rewards were offered to anyone betraying a hidden soldier. One poor woman, tempted by the reward, gave up a soldier and went to the Kommandanteur for her reward. She was later discovered with a knife in her back to which was pinned a piece of paper marked *"Traîtresse"*. Nevertheless there were repeated stories of treachery which made us keener than ever to get out of the district and on our way.

While many plans for our escape were under discussion, it was clear that for any of them to be successful we would require some sort of false papers for crossing France. This was no easy matter. Identification cards were issued centrally in the town, but before one could get one, stamped passport photographs were required. Sally had somehow procured an official German rubber stamp with the eagle across the centre, so we could probably forge the back of the photographs—if we had photographs.

In the end it was decided that the risk must be taken and accordingly one day Sally, Anne Marie and I climbed into Sally's car and set off for the Bon Marché store where there was a photo kiosk. I wore a Red Cross arm band but I was quite sure that if I was stopped and questioned I should be so petrified I would give the game away. After being shut away for so long, the prospect of the simplest of acts like walking down a crowded street was an agony for me. It was bad enough in the car as we drove past the Opera House and the Carlton Hotel, so well known to us in happier times earlier in the year. When we stopped in a side street at the other side of the Grande Place, however, and I had to get out and walk I was trembling with fright. There were Germans everywhere and I was seized with the most unreasonable feeling that I might be recognized by one of my former guards.

We slipped into the store by a side door and pushed our way down the alleys between counters until we came to the two little automatic photograph booths. There was a small queue waiting their turn, so we had to hang about and try to look unconcerned while German troops pushed by. Sally was splendid. She chattered away unconcernedly while I, ashen faced and not daring to look right or left, just nodded my head from time to time, whether I understood what she had said or not.

When my turn came and my photograph was taken it was not the end of the ordeal. We had to wait for twenty minutes while it was developed, so we wandered round the store mingling with other shoppers. I felt that everybody was watching us and noting our movements. At one point to add realism I picked up a bottle of ink and examined it closely. Immediately I was pounced upon by a sales girl who told me in rapid French what the price was and asked me if I wanted it. I immediately panicked and rapidly replaced the bottle without a word. I felt foolish and more conspicuous than ever.

We got back to the machine just as our film was ready and then made all speed back to the car. I did not feel really safe again until I was back behind Sally's front door and drew no comfort from the thought that Johnnie would have to go through the same agony half an hour later.

Sally managed to get us identity cards a few days afterwards, through one of her influential friends, but our joy was short lived. We had only had them a week when we heard that the Germans had found out that there were a lot of forged cards in circulation and ordered all issued after a certain date to be withdrawn. These included ours, so all our risks had been for nothing.

Soon afterwards there was worse news. It became known that the Germans were stepping up their efforts to trace escapers and that house-to-house searches were being conducted. This caused quite a crisis in our household and we had to make a plan for an escape route if the worst happened. There was only one route for us, which involved climbing over the high wall of the back yard into the next garden and this in turn meant taking our neighbour into our confidence. Accordingly she was invited in one evening for a discussion. She proved a good friend and set our minds at rest by telling us that she had sheltered escaping French soldiers during the Great War. We never did have to run for it but it was comforting to know that we had a way out if needed.

By mid-September the food position even for our household was becoming really serious and Sally was finding it impossible to get enough to feed us. However she had a brain wave and one day went off to see our pig merchant friend Monsieur Vaubeck in Pont Thibault. Generous as ever, he there and then killed a pig for us which Sally smuggled back in the boot of her car. We ate portions of that pig twice a day for a fortnight, until I thought that I should never be able to face pork again. The situation was made more tolerable by the fact that there was no shortage of cheap wine and we drank a bottle or so with every meal. Champagne and expensive wines were quite unobtainable as they all went to the Germans but we fared reasonably well on an Algerian red wine which Georges could obtain in apparently limitless quantities.

As I have mentioned, our greatest comfort was the wireless which we kept switched on for most of the day. In the evenings it was jammed by the Germans but during the daytime reception was very good and we listened to every news bulletin with the greatest attention. It was amusing to compare the British version of the course of the war with the German-censored version in the French paper which Georges brought home every evening. The paper, with its slanted news, used to drive Georges to the verge of apoplexy. Sometimes it made him so angry that he would tear it to shreds with much gesticulation.

When Neville Chamberlain died the French papers were

particularly vitriolic, describing him as a "War monger" and "public enemy number one". No effort was spared trying to turn the French people against the British, but if Georges' atittude was anything to go by they did not achieve much success.

September turned into October and there was still no definite news of an escape route. Georges, who was leaving everything to Sally, was becoming fidgety and depressed. He was as anxious as we were to get away and his irritable outbursts of frustration became more and more frequent.

One morning while we were upstairs in our bedrooms he came into the room in a great state of agitation. He never visited us upstairs during the day so we guessed there was some special reason. For a time he paced up and down the room. Then he burst out.

"I cannot bear this any longer. Sally is not getting anywhere. I am going to make some enquiries on my own." He begged us not to say anything of his plans to Sally as it would upset her, so we promised and waited to see what the outcome would be. It was not to be a long wait.

Georges went out immediately after talking to us and returned again at lunchtime as usual but not his usual self. As soon as Sally had gone out he told us with great emotion that he had managed to contact a new organization through some friends in the town. They also claimed to have a way of flying out escapees but with the difference that it first required a long journey to another part of France. He also told us that there was a waiting list of over a thousand and, as they could only take twenty or thirty at a time, there would be a long wait. Just the same Georges felt he was on to something concrete and begged us to trust him.

Our turn came more quickly than we expected. Less than a week later two strangers paid us a call. One was an elderly lady and the other a young flapper. It was the old lady who did all the talking. She had come, she told us, to prepare us for the first part of our journey. From her bag she produced two Polish Passports, one for each of us, and instructed us to paste our photographs into the space provided and do the best we could to forge the official stamp. She left after about a quarter of an hour and we looked at the passports she had left us in dismay. Compared with our French "*cartes d'identité*" they were very crude indeed and unlikely to deceive anybody.

We were now very upset and found it hard to obey Georges' instructions not to tell Sally the news. He was determined that she should only know at the last moment so that she would not have an opportunity to talk us out of it. Meantime he assured us that we would be collected in three days' time.

It was agreed that Sally should be told on the night prior to our departure and at dinner we timidly broke the news. At first she would not believe it and simply laughed. Then when we convinced her that we were serious, her French temperament took over. She rushed about the room in floods of tears, wringing her hands. She begged us to change our minds and not trust ourselves to two casual acquaintances and an organization about which she knew nothing. We felt desperately sorry for her but now that the first real chance of escape had appeared we were not to be moved.

Finding us adamant she then turned on Georges and cursed him for his duplicity but he too would not give an inch.

When she saw that we were all determined to go through with the plan, she gave in and set about preparing us as best she could for the next day's journey.

Chapter 6

I can well understand why long-term prisoners feel reluctant to face the world again when finally they come to the end of their sentences and are released. Although I had fretted during the long weeks when we had been confined, now that the moment had come for action I shrank from it with something very like fear. Suddenly the big, square house seemed terribly safe, comfortable and infinitely desirable. Outside was the unknown, perilous and menacing.

I awoke early and peeped through the curtains of my bedroom window. At least it was a fine day with the first shafts of sunlight starting to break through the morning mist. I dressed carefully, trying on my French beret at several angles in an attempt to hit off exactly the right degree of nonchalance. I fiddled with my tie and looked at myself in the mirror over and over again. Finally I went downstairs and waited in a state of considerable nervousness for the rest of the household to join me.

Zero hour, when we were to leave the house, was set for 2 pm. That morning was ghastly. Sally rushed around the house like a clucking hen with her chicks. Two suitcases were produced for the three of us, in which we packed our few belongings. Georges presented Johnnie and me with some underclothes and shirts of his own as spares. He himself appropriated the largest suitcase and, while we watched with dismay, carefully packed his uniform! This seemed to me to be the height of folly and would invite awkward questions if our baggage was searched. I tried to persuade him to leave it behind but he was determined and nothing I could say had the slightest effect.

We had an early lunch. Somehow Sally had managed a wonderful spread as a farewell feast but the meat, procured at goodness knows what cost, stuck in my throat. I struggled manfully to do justice to her efforts, conscious that we had no idea when we would eat again, but it was no good. Half way through I had to excuse myself hurriedly and made a bolt for the lavatory where I threw it all up. Johnnie, I could see, was managing little better and poor Sally was perhaps in the greatest state of nerves of all of us. Only Georges munched away contentedly as if he had not a care in the world.

During the morning a simple plan had been made for leaving the house. The old lady whom we had met a few days before was to act as our guide. Georges and Maroc, who was not going to be left behind, were to leave with the guide carrying the suitcases as if they were going on a normal trip. Johnnie and I were to drive with Sally close behind.

The old lady arrived exactly on time. We watched through the windows as the walkers set off. The lady guide in front, Georges following about thirty yards behind and Maroc, always the perfect servant, a few paces behind him. As soon as they turned the corner of the street, and we were satisfied that their departure had created no suspicion, we climbed into the car and set off in pursuit.

At this stage none of us had, of course, the slightest idea where the guide was leading us but it soon became more and more obvious that we were heading for the railway station. This made Sally's agitation even greater. She knew that all the trains were crowded with German soldiers, either travelling on duty or going on leave, and that they were

111

regularly searched. Stopping the car, she begged us to re-consider putting our trust in a plan of escape of which we knew nothing and return with her to the house. I for one was tempted to listen to her pleas, but now that we were started it seemed impossibly cowardly to turn back. Finally she drove us to the main thoroughfare by the Grande Place where she stopped under a tree and we both got out. The final farewell was painful but brief. She kissed us both goodbye and drove off quickly so that we should not see her tears. We were near to that state ourselves. As her car was swallowed up in the traffic we felt terribly alone. During the weeks we had been under her roof we had grown very close —how close we only now realized.

We had to hurry to catch up with our guide, who had drawn well ahead of us. As on my previous excursion in the open streets, I felt myself to be the centre of all eyes. Surely one of the many uniformed Germans who crowded the pavements must see through our amateurish disguise. I hardly dared to raise my eyes from the ground, only glanc-ing up every now and again to keep the old lady in sight, so that in my haste I kept bumping into people which made my confusion all the more complete.

Eventually we arrived outside the station but the old lady kept on down a little side street where she suddenly dived into a working-man's cafe. We followed her and almost fell over the feet of two German soldiers, sprawled at a table inside the door. Georges took his seat at a vacant table at the far end of the room while the respectful Maroc seated himself a few tables away. Georges was magnificent. While the Germans stared at us curiously he ordered us coffee and started a rapid, rather one-sided conversation. The old lady sipped her coffee in a leisurely manner and then got up and left. The Germans were by this time deeply involved in their own conversation and Georges was able to indicate to us that we should stay where we were. His own unconcern and the presence of Maroc who was grinning away happily at some private joke of his own helped to calm our shaky nerves so that when the old lady returned and indicated that this time we should follow her we were in a much more composed frame of mind.

Mingling with the crowds which were milling round the booking office we felt much less conspicuous and, although we clung closely to Georges' coat-tails, we were already beginning to gain confidence in our new-found freedom—a confidence which was to grow with the events of the next few minutes.

First the old lady nudged a railway official who turned and smiled at Georges. Then she nodded to us casually and disappeared into the crowds. Her part in the operation was finished and we were never to see her again. Our new guide, for that was who he turned out to be, now boldly cleared a way for us through the masses of people until he brought us up against the platform barrier. He bent down and whispered something to the ticket collector who nodded and, ignoring the waiting queue of travellers, signed to us to pass through. He then escorted us up the whole length of the train to a carriage close behind the engine where we were met by yet another uniformed official who was evidently the guard of the train. The first official kissed Georges warmly on both cheeks in true French style and departed so that we realized that we had been handed over to yet another member of the organization.

Everything had gone like clockwork and we felt that we were in the hands of a really well-organized team. To our further surprise we found that four seats had been reserved for us—a difficult thing to achieve in such conditions—and we took our places feeling more like V.I.P.s than men on the run carrying forged documents.

113

There were still ten minutes to pass before the train started and soon it was standing room only. A crowd of German soldiers entered but made no attempt, as I feared they might, to turn us out of our seats. Nor did Georges make any move to give up his seat when some elderly women carrying heavy baskets crushed into our compartment and we, feeling rather ungallant, took our example from him. Instead we concealed ourselves behind our papers and speculated with some trepidation on what might be our destination. Then the train with much huffing and puffing pulled out of the station and the next stage in our adventures had begun.

Now that I had time to relax I began to reflect on the strangeness, not to say the absurdity, of our situation. For weeks past we had been concealed in the various houses of our resistance friends in Lille and on the farms, fearful with every knock at the door that our refuge had been discovered. Prior to that again we had lived like fugitives from justice against whom we had felt that every man's hand was turned, moving by night and lying up by day, living on what we could scrounge and unwilling to let ourselves be glimpsed by even the most simple country yokel. Now here we were in broad daylight, surrounded by people and being carried every minute, we assumed, nearer to freedom.

It was a Gilbertian situation which I could not believe could last for long. At every station I expected to get a signal from our friend the guard to disembark and to be thrown back once more on our own resources. I knew Johnnie must be troubled by the same thoughts. I glanced at him from behind my paper. With his blonde hair and blue eyes he looked more out of place than anyone I could imagine. To add to his confusion, the old peasant woman sitting next to him was knitting away industriously but every now and again her ball of wool would fall off her lap on to the carriage floor; then everyone would scramble about trying to retrieve it for her and compliments would be exchanged in voluble French. Poor Johnnie was obviously terrified that, if he joined in the general mêlée, he would be drawn into conversation so he tried to pretend that he did not notice and shrank deeper into his corner in an effort to achieve invisibility. While I was watching this charade with amusement, Georges suddenly leant across, tapped me on the knee and cupping his hand to my ear whispered the one word, "Paris".

In my astonishment I almost exclaimed out loud. Surely he could not mean that we were headed for Paris, by all accounts seething with Germans and subject to the strictest security checks! While I was trying to reconcile myself to the enormity of this idea, another nagging thought crossed my mind; to get to Paris we had to cross the Somme which was on the frontier between the *Zone Interdit* and the remainder of occupied France. In my intensive study of possible escape routes I had learned that the crossing of this frontier was forbidden to civilians without special permits. The prohibited zone had been formed to prevent the majority of the French public from knowing details of the German invasion build-up and it was more difficult to obtain permits for it even than for Unoccupied France. I had imagined that we would have left the train long before this point and would have to find our way across at night on our flat feet. I could only trust that Georges' people knew what they were doing.

We passed through Arras, the location of the old G.H.Q. of the British Expeditionary Force, and then pressed on further south to Amiens. At some point I may have dozed off briefly, for when I awoke, everyone in the carriage was rummaging in pockets or opening bags looking for their tickets. As the train slowed to a halt I looked across at

115

Georges but he was making no attempt to follow the example of our fellow travellers. He just sat there unconcernedly gazing into space. I thought of my pathetically inadequate identification papers and wondered what on earth he had up his sleeve.

In fact when the guard came to our compartment the whole thing was ludicrously simple. Everybody else's documents were examined with scrupulous care, but when he came to us, Georges simply slipped something into his hand and he gave Georges a broad wink and retired. Later I asked Georges what the miraculous *laissez passer* had been. "I gave him a 500 franc note," George said airily.

You can have no idea what tremendous confidence this incident inspired in us. As the train gathered speed again out of Amiens station I felt that there was nothing that was impossible to the organisation into whose hands we had so happily fallen. Everything would be taken care of and all we had to do was play the game of follow-my-leader with the incredible Georges. In a few days we would, I now began to assume, be wafted across the border into Unoccupied France and our troubles would be at an end. How we were to escape from the Unoccupied Zone, if this indeed was our destination, was, in my state of elation, only a minor detail. In anticipation I was already imagining the joy of reunion with my parents, the surprise of my fellow officers and the ineffable delight of being once more safely back in Britain. Thus I floated on a rosy cloud nearer and nearer to Paris.

We had left Lille at 3 pm and it was almost exactly 10 pm when the train pulled into the Gare du Nord. We climbed stiffly out on to the dark platform and, mingling with the crowd, passed without trouble through the barrier. Up to this point Georges had had no opportunity of explaining to us the outline of the plan we were to follow.

Now we learned that we were to make for a rendezvous with another agent at a certain cross-roads at the other side of Paris. As it was already past 10 pm and the curfew came into force at 11 pm there was no time to lose. We bought our two franc tickets for the metro as the quickest and easiest method of transport. There were not many people about at this late hour and the trains were few and far between so that it was almost ten minutes to eleven when we arrived at our destination and raced up the stairs into the blacked-out street.

After the trepidation with which I had started out on our travels that morning I was now beginning to enter into the spirit of things almost with joy and was looking forward to seeing what sort of person our new guide might turn out to be and where he or she had arranged for us to spend the night. We were in for a shock.

When we arrived at our rendezvous there was nobody there! The cross-roads were completely deserted. Nothing stirred in any direction. It was as quiet and dark as the grave. Georges examined his watch and meticulously checked his directions. There was no doubt that we were in the right place and if anyone was hiding in the shadow they could hardly mistake us as we stood together in an irresolute group. For a few minutes nobody spoke and then one after another all over Paris the clocks started to chime the curfew hour. As the sound died away Georges started to laugh and we joined him. Suddenly it seemed to us all that the situation was ludicrous rather than precarious. Perhaps it was the reaction after the long, tense day. Anyway there we were with no idea at all what to do, standing in the middle of the road shaking with laughter as if we had not a care in the world.

It was quite a few minutes before we pulled ourselves together sufficiently to face up to the necessity for some sort of action. At least we were in a quiet, deserted part of Paris but at any moment a patrol car might come past, so it was desperately urgent to find a refuge for the night. We were trying to decide which road to take when we spotted far down one street the very faint blur of a dim lamp. It was as good a choice as any so we set off in that direction. It turned out to be an hotel and, without more ado, Georges marched inside while we trailed along behind him. The manageress was a kindly-looking provincial lady. "Yes," she answered to Georges question, she had rooms for us. "Could I just see your papers?" It was what I was dreading. Johnnie's passport gave his age as thirty-three while with his baby face he loked scarcely out of his teens. Mine was slightly more probable but I certainly did not imagine that my description as a thirty-five-year-old Polish refugee called Joseph Karensky was going to fool anyone, least of all this discerning old lady. Georges showed his papers first which were, of course, in perfect order as were Maroc's. Then it was my turn. She took one look at the strange Polish document, grinned and handed it back to me. "Follow me," she said, "I will show you to your rooms." This had certainly been our lucky day.

We awoke the following morning in a less light-hearted mood than the night before. Our situation was now worse than when he had been comfortably esconced in Lille. There at least we had friends who were working on plans for our escape. Here in Paris we were cut off from the underground due to the failure of a link in the organization. Worse, we would now have to survive in the open without proper identity documents and without even ration cards so that we could eat. Johnnie and I discussed this dismal position in the room which we shared. We were interrupted by the arrival of Georges, who burst in on us dressed, to our horror, in his full uniform! While we had been discussing how to get by in Paris without drawing attention to ourselves here was the bold Georges, himself listed by the Germans as an ex officer confined to the Lille area, apparently determined to be as conspicuous as possible. Moreover he had decided to go out immediately to try and contact someone he knew of in Deuxième Bureau through whom he was sure he would be able to pick up the thread of our escape route again. The hotel did not serve meals and as we had not eaten since the previous day we were ravenous, but when we mentioned the matter to Georges he brushed it aside as being of no account. It would be impossible to eat until he had found somewhere where they did not demand ration cards and, as it was Sunday, he did not expect to have much success in this direction until the following day. Then, making us promise not to leave the hotel until he returned, he gave us a carefree wave of his hand and strode out into the street.

By midday Georges was back, his usual imperturbable attitude to life severely shaken. In fact he was in such a furious temper that it was some time before he was coherent enough to tell us what had happened. It appeared that he had called at the Deuxième Bureau to be told the man would be in later. After a wait of two hours he appeared and Georges set about questioning him to find out what had gone wrong the previous evening. At first the man pretended to know nothing about it, although Georges had been given his name as a contact before leaving Lille. Georges got the impression that he knew about the organisation but was, for some reason, unwilling to admit it. After about ten minutes of conversation, however, he was caught out on a point and was then forced to admit that it was he who had failed us. He explained that the Germans were getting suspicious and that he was no longer prepared to take risks. Georges, his patriotism fully on the boil, was so angry that it was all he could do to stop himself from striking the wretched Surete official. Did he not realize, he asked him, that by breaking the chain, he was endangering not only our chances of escape but was wrecking the escape route for those who were following on behind us? In the end Georges got a certain amount of satisfaction by extracting a promise that the man would at least inform the organization in the north of France that their plans had crashed at the Paris end.

Another piece of information that Georges extracted was that previous escapees to Britain had been flown out in a light aircraft which had been landed in a remote part of Le Bourget airport. However improbable this seemed it did at least confirm the story we had heard ourselves in Lille. At any event this bold scheme now lay in ruins and we were thrown back on our own resources.

It was at this stage that Johnnie's and my thoughts turned to the American Embassy. America was, of course, not yet in the war and preserved her diplomatic relations with Germany. We could not believe, however, if we threw ourselves on their mercy that there would not be some way in which they could help us. Georges, whose spirits were temporarily at a low ebb, cheered up immensely at the thought and immediately adopted the idea as his own. He insisted that he set off again at once to make contact despite the fact that it was Sunday.

He returned two hours later to report that there were indeed no officials on duty but that he had met the doorman who had assured him that we would certainly get a hearing. By this time Johnnie and I were so fed up with waiting and starving in our little room that we could stay inactive no longer. In spite of Georges' protests we declared that we must have some food and that later we would pay a visit to the American Embassy ourselves. Accordingly the three of us set off together, first giving Maroc some money so that he too could eat. Our mouths watering in anticipation to an extent which made caution a second consideration, we went in search of a cafe.

We found one in the corner of a large square. At first they said that they could only supply us with dry bread; then, as an afterthought, they added that of course we could have some wine and oysters which were not rationed. I do not remember ever enjoying a meal so much! I have worshipped the oyster ever since.

Georges' acquaintance at the American Embassy turned out to be an extremely placid individual, apparently not at all surprised to hear that we were British officers on the run. Many British, he told us, called at the Embassy but whether they were soldiers or civilians seeking exit permits he could not say. All he could do was to assure us, that if we called the next day, he would see to it that we got to the right official without having to wait in the inevitable queue. With that we had to be, for the meantime, content.

In Paris that afternoon the sun was shining and the trees were gay with autumn tints. Only the people we passed wore hang-dog expressions and shuffled about their business in a listless way. Georges was deeply upset and kept repeating. *"Paris est triste, c'est terrible."* Then in a burst of anger he said in English, "Seeing the Germans in Paris is like finding a man in bed with my wife!" We felt desperately sorry for him.

Quite resigned we walked about together. Even with Georges dressed in his preposterous uniform we felt quite safe and certain that no one would stop us for our identity cards. I did not know Paris well, having only paid brief visits on my way to and from Switzerland before the war, but I felt that all the *joie de vivre* which had made her an irresistible attraction to the British tourist had shrivelled and

121

died. The Hotel Crillon, which occupies much of one side of the Place de la Concorde and which was near the American Embassy, was draped with numerous black and red swastika flags. Sentries paced up and down outside it and the pavement was lined with grey-painted staff cars. Indeed there was no civilian traffic, only German cars and lorries and very few civilians walking the streets.

We crossed into the Tuileries Gardens which, to our delight, were fairly empty. A few German soldiers strolled with their Parisian girl friends. We passed one photographing his companion just as the camera clicked and we wondered what he would think if he knew he had recorded in the background of his picture two very frightened British escapees.

As darkness started to fall we returned to our cafe for some more oysters and then rejoined Maroc in the hotel. He was as cheerful as ever and had managed to find some bread and cheese in a friendly cafe to sustain him. His Moslem religion stood him in good stead. His belief in Kismet was absolute. Allah would provide all his needs and if Allah wished him to come to any harm there was nothing he could do to prevent it.

The following morning we were at the Embassy early but already a considerable crowd had collected which formed a queue stretching into the road outside. A few people muttered angrily as we pushed to the front. By good fortune we caught the eye of our friend who, as good as his word, steered us into a private waiting room and left us saying that he would see somebody was told of our presence. This appeared to be the extent of his influence for we now waited for several hours in an increasing state of anxiety but nobody came. Finally as we were wondering if in fact anybody knew we were there at all, a tall, well-dressed American put his head round the door and was obviously very surprised to see us. He asked what we wanted and, feeling it was the only hope, we told him our full story fully and frankly. Poor man, he was completely overwhelmed and had obviously never come across a similar problem before. It was at this point that he suddenly remembered that there was an elderly Englishman working somewhere in the Embassy building whom, he was sure, would give us help and advice.

This was good news but our hearts sank when we were shown to a seat in the corner of the man's office. He was dealing with a terrified Cypriot woman who wanted to be returned to her homeland and it was clear to me that he was a broken reed. This was quickly confirmed when it came to our turn. He listened briefly to what I had to say and then launched into an interminable diatribe about his own troubles. It was a disgrace, he said, that the Germans should not allow a man of his age to return to England. Having made this point he then told us his own military career. After a time we realized that he was not talking about his service in this current war nor even the Great War, but in the South African campaign!

I am afraid I interrupted him rather abruptly and insisted that he listen to our problems instead of treating us as if we were paying him a social call. He was quite hurt but it did not take him long to explain to us, as we had anticipated, that he could do nothing. Our most urgent need was for money so that we could help ourselves, but this appeared to be the most difficult thing of all. There had been a time when the Americans had been prepared to advance money to such as us but this had now been stopped. Once more we had come to a dead end.

That afternoon we continued our wandering through the streets of Paris. Somehow we felt far safer mingling with the Parisian crowds than we had done on our tentative outings in Lille. Now that we were becoming used to not being cooped up we were quite exhilarated by the range of freedom. If only Georges would not wear his damned uniform! We made our way to the Place de l'Opera which was crowded with people apparently as aimless as we were. Georges marched on ahead while we followed behind. With the disparity in our ages we might have been on an outing with our father. We soon began to notice that people were turning to look at Georges, nudging each other as he passed. In truth he could not have been more conspicuous if he had tried and it really began to worry us. Then, to our amazement, as we turned a corner, we came face to face with another middle-aged French officer in full uniform walking towards us. As the two old gentlemen passed each other they swept their arms up in salute, without the slightest facial expression or alteration of their pace. For a moment it seemed that France had never fallen and that there were no Germans thronging the street. It was really rather magnificent. This was the only other Frenchman we saw during the whole time we were in Paris who had dared to wear his uniform.

Georges seemed quite unaware of our misery and continued his majestic way. The more people stared, including the German soldiers, the more he puffed out his chest and the more military his bearing became. It was, it seemed to us, sheer madness and it was not until some time later that we managed to persuade him to stop off at a cafe where we sought out the least conspicuous seats we could find. There was a trolley of sticky cakes being pushed around between the tables and, discovering that no coupons were required, we set about a meal, bought with our few remaining francs, that would have brought joy to the heart of a schoolboy. Our enjoyment was only slightly spoiled when two German N.C.O.s sat down at the next table and, with a clanking of bayonet scabbards, took off their belts and dropped them at our feet. They appeared, however, to be interested only in the beer and took no notice of our odd party.

It was in the middle of this feast that Georges suddenly had another idea. He was always having ideas! He whispered that he had someone to see and swept out into the street again, with us following obediently in his wake.

It turned out that he had remembered that before the war he had been extremely friendly with a senior executive of the French newspaper, *Le Matin*. Leaving us pretending an interest in the photographs in their windows, he strode into the newspaper offices. We had an uncomfortable wait before he finally appeared again and from the look on his face we quickly gathered that his idea had not been fruitful. We later learned that he had hoped, on the basis of his old friendship, to get a loan. To his unutterable disgust the man turned out to be completely unco-operative and had shown Georges the door in no uncertain manner.

So another day passed with no progress made. We did get a little satisfaction, however, on our way back to the hotel, when Georges turned into a tailor's shop and ordered a row of medal ribbons which he could sew on to his civilian suit. Our protests had not been in vain and we did not see the uniform again after that day. Although it had frightened us at the time I have subsequently thought that perhaps, after all, his uniform was not a bad cover. Nobody with anything to hide would have been mad enough to wear it!

Next morning we were up again bright and early, determined once more to see if we could get a proper hearing at the American Embassy. As we hurried from the metro station to our destination there was a guttural shout behind us and, when we turned, to our horror we saw a German sentry advancing purposefully towards us. My first instinct was to make a bolt for it but better sense prevailed and we stood our ground. It appeared that all we had done was inadvertently to cross a military barrier. He pushed us roughly into the correct pedestrian stream and returned to his post. It was a nasty moment and a timely reminder not to be over-confident.

Once inside the Embassy, we fared rather better than the previous day. Our friend on the door ushered us to a vacant office at the far end of the building and almost immediately we found ourselves being interviewed by a friendly American official. That, however, was as far as our luck went. We explained our desperate need for money but drew a complete blank. The Germans had been getting suspicious of the Embassy's activities and the Americans were afraid that their diplomatic privileges might be curtailed if they got any further involved with the likes of us. The American was polite but firm. The answer was "no dice". There was nothing for it but to leave.

It was at this low point in our fortunes that our Guardian Angel, whose absence had been conspicuous during the last two days, suddenly made a timely re-appearance. We were wandering disconsolately towards the exit to the Embassy when we were stopped by a neatly-dressed, middle-aged lady who said to us in English: "I hear that you are escapees and need some help." Before we could recover from our surprise she had bundled us into an empty office and started to ply us with pointed questions. Hearing that we had a Frenchman with us and that he was waiting in the hall Georges was sent for and thereafter, for better security, the conversation was conducted in French.

Our rescuer's name was Kitty Bonnefous, an English-woman married to a Frenchman. She had an air of direct-ness and determination which did much to reassure us. When we told her that we had been refused money she was highly indignant and immediately offered to do battle for us

126

herself. She made it clear that this was not the first time that she had come across a situation like ours. When we parted company about a quarter of an hour later matters were already under way. We were to go to her flat that afternoon for a full-scale council of war and meantime she would do what she could to get the money.

It was a highly elated trio who stepped out again into the sunlight of the Place de la Concorde. With six hours to kill before our appointment we once more set off on our sightseeing walks. In the Rue de Rivoli we stopped to look in the windows of the many curio and antique shops. It was remarkable how unaffected they seemed to be by the occupation. They displayed big stocks of expensive articles and appeared to be doing a good trade. It was only in the restaurants and the cafes that the disaster which had befallen Paris was evident. In the Place de l'Opera we once more fell foul of a German sentry by wandering on to forbidden ground on the pavement outside one of the many big buildings they had taken over as administrative offices. Snarling with rage he kicked and shoved us into the gutter while the passing Parisians sniggered at our discomfiture. We walked away as quickly as possible with our tails between our legs.

The arrogance of the Germans in Paris was everywhere noticeable. Even more offensive to us were the posters which were stuck up on every hoarding displaying vitriolic anti-British propaganda. Only a month before the British had sunk part of the French fleet at Oran and this was being made much of to convince the French that the British were their real enemies. A certain poster I remember depicted a French sailor drowning in the sea, holding a tricolor aloft, with the words "*N'oubliez pas Oran*" printed beneath. The German propaganda machine would have had more chance of success if their own behaviour in Paris had been better. Instead they constantly infuriated the ordinary citizen with their domineering attitude and their obvious conviction that they were the Master Race.

A little incident sticks pleasurably in my mind. As we were reading one of the many German propaganda posters, a Frenchman and his wife also stopped to read. The man made some strongly derogatory remark and spat deliberately on the ground to show his contempt before walking on. His attitude, I am sure, reflected the attitude of most decent people.

I was later to discuss this subject with Kitty. She said that the great majority of the French were loyal but warned us that there were a few who would betray us at the slightest excuse. Immediately after the fall of Paris there had been a great deal of apathy which was understandable when the situation looked so hopeless. Now, however, people were beginning to recover their spirits and were developing a healthy loathing for the Germans. It only needed the slightest encouragement from the British to stiffen their opposition still further. For example, a few days before our arrival a solitary British aircraft had flown over the city and traced out the word "Courage" in smoke. That single act did much to destroy, in a few minutes, months of German propaganda.

The rest of that morning we spent visiting Notre Dame. It was infested with Germans. Outside, troop-carrying lorries were drawn up and every few minutes a new party, accompanied by a French guide, was marched into the Cathedral to absorb their ration of "*Kultur*". We followed respectfully in the wake of one large party and spent almost an hour studying the beauties of the sculptures and stained glass.

The time seemed interminable until the hour when we were due at Kitty's but it finally arrived and we set off in the metro with a feeling of excitement. Of course, in our

128

14 The Reverend Donald Caskie, who ran the Marseilles Mission to Seamen, outside the Scots Church in Paris.

15 Benjamin Slor with whom the author escaped from Marseilles to Jerusalem.

anxiety, we arrived early but we were at once admitted by a smart maid in apron and cap. Kitty's first words were, "You must be starving!" and at once an enormous spread of cakes and buns was laid before us as well as a big plateful each of bacon and eggs. I felt like the starving man in one of Sapper's short stories who, in like circumstances, prayed under his breath; "God! Let me eat like a gentleman!" It was some time before we finally cleared the table and got down to business.

Kitty was nothing if not practical. She was a woman of about fifty who came from a solid, middle-class, English background and who for many years had been married to a prominent Bordeaux wine merchant. They were now living apart although they remained on friendly terms. I have already mentioned that Kitty had the effect of inspiring us with instant confidence, such was her directness of manner and forceful personality. We were rather surprised, therefore, to find that she had a companion staying with her in the flat who was quite the opposite. This was a woman called Etta Shiber who was an American and who, it seemed, was in some way connected with Kitty's work for the Underground. She was a bundle of nerves and, although she attended our discussions with Kitty, was clearly something of an irritation and an embarrassment to her.

Much later I was to hear that Mrs Shiber was arrested by the Germans on a charge of helping the enemy but was repatriated to America in exchange for a German the Americans had arrested.

It was our supreme good luck to have been found by Kitty when she was doing the heroic job for which she was later to suffer so much. She was working officially for the Croix Rouge, much as Sally was doing in Lille, and in this capacity she travelled long distances outside Paris in her 402 Peugeot, visiting hospitals, caring for British and

129

French wounded. This activity provided her with an excellent cover for the secret side of her work which was helping British P.O.W.s to escape. To get extra petrol for her unscheduled journies she traded bars of chocolates with the German storekeepers.

In the course of conversation she mentioned that one of the camps she visited regularly was Doullens where, it will be remembered, both Johnnie and I had been for a time and where I had left Colin Hunter recovering from his eye wound. She had already helped six British Officers to escape from there and I asked her out of curiosity if she could remember any of their names. The first one she mentioned was Colin!

Whilst visiting the wards she met Colin and tipped him off to go out to her car in the park and hide in the boot. This he did successfully and Kitty drove him through to her flat in Paris without incident. Encouraged by her easy passage with Colin, Kitty gave the same instructions to a corporal in the Buffs, Hood Cree by name, on her next visit to Doullens. He was over six feet tall and the boot was small so it could only be a temporary expedient as a hiding place. To add to his difficulties he was recovering from a severe leg wound. In squeezing into his cramped quarters the poor chap had got his bad leg jammed under the cushion of the back seat, pushing it out of position.

Unfortunately when Kitty stopped clear of the hospital to let him out she was descended upon by a large, fat German officer demanding a lift. He got into the back before she could stop him. She was in no position to refuse or move him and so drove him for thirty miles in an agony of suspense that the protruding limb might be discovered. The sufferings of the poor invalid in the boot can be imagined.

Later, having dropped her unwanted passenger, as she was approaching the gates of Paris, she had a puncture.

The spare wheel was in the boot, so Hood Cree had to be extracted to get it out. Together they set about changing the wheel. There was an ugly moment when another German officer pulled up, this time offering help, but Kitty was able to side-track him and assure him that the job was almost finished.

These tales of her various activities convinced us that we had struck gold and could trust her completely.

Her plan, like the one for our departure from Lille, was bold and simple. Her husband was an influential man who still had substantial interests in Bordeaux. Between them they had established an escape route right down into unoccupied France. The first step was for her to buy us tickets on a train to a small town near Bordeaux where we would be met by her agent and guided to a point where we could step across into the Free French Zone. It was the route which others had taken, including my friend Colin, and no one had so far run into trouble. It was too late to start that night and anyway the agent had to be alerted so it was agreed that we return to our hotel once more and make a start in the morning. As we left she pressed a thousand franc note into Georges' hand. She explained that it was not her money. She had bullied it out of an American official after we had left the Embassy that morning!

We left the flat in the highest of spirits and Georges decided that we really deserved to stand ourselves a celebration dinner. As he was expecting some mysterious message to arrive by train from the North, we set off for the Gare du Nord. There was no message so we sought out a large restaurant near the station and called for the manager. Georges delicately explained our position about coupons to him and the medal ribbons on his chest did the rest. He treated us as honoured guests and hovered round us while we ate what he was able to produce. It consisted of soup, a dish of eels and a heavy bread pudding. Not perhaps what we would have ordered if we had had a free choice, and it cost us almost two pounds a head.

Back once more in our little hotel the manageress told us that she thought the French Police were on our track. They already knew more about us than was healthy and she did not think it would be safe for us to stay there after that night. It was quite obvious that she had known all the time that we were not what we pretended to be. She was just another of those splendid people on whom the safety of our journeying through France depended. When we told her that we would be gone in the morning, she was greatly relieved. The faithful Maroc, too, was overjoyed when we told him that by nightfall the next day we hoped to be several hundred miles nearer his beloved country.

That night I slept ill. In spite of my great confidence in Kitty I could not help wondering what perils were in store for us. From the way Johnnie was tossing and turning in the next bed I knew that his thoughts were following the same lines.

Chapter 7

The following morning we lay in bed late. There was no point in making ourselves more conspicuous than we needed now that the next stage in our journey was planned.

We were all invited to lunch with Kitty so we set out at around midday. It was another splendid meal of which we took full advantage, for we had no idea when we should eat in such civilized surroundings again—nor, indeed, when we should eat at all.

Georges left early to collect Maroc and our luggage from the hotel and Johnnie and I were driven to the Gare de Lyon by Kitty—to arrive twenty minutes before the time of departure. We had only known Kitty a matter of hours but parting from her was a wrench. We both embraced her warmly and walked quickly into the station.

The train was already in the platform and we were glad to see it was far from full. Up near the engine we found an empty compartment. We dumped our things and then stood outside on the platform waiting anxiously for Georges and Maroc to put in an appearance. The train was in blackness and as we hovered by the carriage door we heard a purposeful military tramping coming down the corridor. We scuttled back to our compartment and a moment later the dim figure of a German soldier was silhouetted in the doorway. We cowered back in our seats while he swept the compartment with his torch. We felt sure he was going to question us but he was merely checking that the windows were blacked out and with a curt nod passed on his way. When we plucked up courage once again to move out and stand on the platform we saw Georges and Maroc coming towards us.

The journey passed uneventfully. Only one other traveller got into our compartment a few stations down the line and he got out again about an hour before we reached our destination.

The train pulled into Libourne, a fair-sized town some twenty-five kilometres east of Bordeaux at four in the morning. Our instructions were to make our way to the station hotel where the night porter, we had been told, would let us lie up until daylight. We arrived shivering with cold and half-asleep. The porter showed us into the dining-room and then went off to make us some coffee.

So far everything had gone beautifully, and as we had been told in Paris that the south-west of France was free of occupation troops, the crossing of the frontier appeared a piece of cake. Our spirits were soaring but we were in for yet another shock. Georges explained to the porter that we were strangers and asked for information about the town. He told us that the day before two German regiments had arrived and that at that moment there were thirty German officers snoring upstairs. Now that we knew that the town was garrisoned it seemed certain that we would have to change our plans all over again.

It was quite obvious that it would be unsafe for us to stay where we were after 6 a.m. At the same time the streets were not likely to be much safer. Georges could not approach Kitty's agent until at least nine o'clock, which left us with three hours to kill after leaving the hotel. The rest of the night dragged on and we got more and more worried. Just before six we heard the floor above come to life and a raucous German voice shouted for some service.

After an earnest conference we decided that we should

split up into pairs and walk briskly about the streets to give the impression that we were on our way to work. Georges was to go to the address we had been given and we were to note the house he entered and then return at intervals to keep a lookout for a signal. Our main fear was that the arrival of the German troops would so intimidate our man that he would refuse to co-operate.

We walked all over Libourne as purposefully as we could for three hours, much of the time in the semi-darkness. Happily Georges found the house easily enough and we saw him admitted. Then there followed a ghastly half hour while we walked round and round, up one street and down the other, waiting to see what was going to happen.

At last we got the expected signal and half running, half walking, made for the open front door. Our fears were justified. The agent was a merchant aged between thirty and forty and he was in a complete funk. With much gesticulation he told us that two days ago he would have been only too glad to have helped us, but that the arrival of the Germans made it quite impossible for him. So great was his panic that he would not even hear of our staying in his house for a few hours while we thought what to do. A few minutes later we were once more in the street.

It was the same situation as the one in which we had found ourslves on our arrival in Paris. We were on our own in a strange town, which teemed with Germans and where it was likely that anyone we approached would be in the same state of confusion and fear as the man we had just left. We could do nothing but walk round hoping for some inspiration.

One of the things I remember best about Libourne is the number of public lavatories it boasted. There seemed to be one at every street corner and we took every advantage of them, spending countless francs to rest awhile in the little boxes. It was not only rest we needed, we also used them frequently for the purpose for which they were intended, so great was the strain!

We were now only a few miles from the border but there were German troops everywhere and our chances of making the journey on foot without being challenged was minimal.

By arrangement we all met up again at midday to find that Georges had some good news. Signalling to us to enter a nearby cafe we sat down at a table and he started to explain what we were going to do. Every now and again he was interrupted by squads of Germans marching past, and we stopped talking until they had gone by. However, Georges' new plan was sufficiently feasible that confidence was restored.

Somehow he had met up with a man of Polish extraction who had offered to drive us to the border in his lorry. He would not be ready to make the journey until four in the afternoon but meantime he knew of a warehouse on the banks of the Dordogne where we could lie up and wait for him.

It turned out that the warehouse was a wine store. The door was open and we got in without difficulty. Inside the smell of maturing wine was overpowering. Under the floor and punctuated every ten yards or so with a trap door was a huge storage tank and round the walls the barrels of Bordeaux stood three deep. The fumes were so strong that slowly but surely we got slightly drunk—"zig-zag", to use the graphic French expression.

Our meal of bread and sausage was washed down with tins full of raw red wine dipped into the tank, so we were in fine fettle when, precisely at the appointed hour, we heard a lorry draw up outside the door. In the weeks we had been hunted we had learned caution, so despite our semi-inebriated state, we had the presence of mind to hide behind the barrels until Georges recognized his Polish friend.

Our transport turned out to be not a normal lorry but a wine tanker. Before we left a pipe was run into the warehouse and wine was pumped out until the tanker was full. Then one of the assistants sat on the tank at the back while the driver, another assistant and the four of us all piled into the driver's cabin. It was a fearful crush with poor Maroc having to crouch as best he could on the floor.

After clearing the town we made our way through winding lanes, lined with vines. At each crossroads there was a German motorcyclist on duty and groups of Germans were dotted about the fields. There was no doubt that they were on the lookout for people escaping into Free France and we were doubly glad that we had not attempted the journey on foot.

As we progressed the number of German troops got fewer and fewer so that our hopes began to rise that it would not, after all, be so difficult to find our way across the frontier. We were just thinking that we were getting very near the end of the ride when our Polish friend turned sharply off down a side road and signalled us to dismount. He then led the way down a short track to a farm where we were made welcome by an old lady and her two sons. We had stumbled into the hands of an experienced group who were used to smuggling people across the boundary.

One of the sons beckoned to us to follow him across the fields. Shortly we came to a tarmac road running across our front. On the other side was a five-barred gate painted black and white announcing the fact in French and German that we were at the frontier itself. Matters now became surprisingly simple. It was explained to us that a motorcyclist patrolled the road, passing every ten minutes or so. All we had to do was to lie concealed until he was past and then make a dash for it.

The operation was a push-over. We waited for about ten minutes until the motorcyclist showed up and the moment he disappeared from view we shot across the road, vaulted the gate and kept running as fast and as straight as we could until we were out of breath. We were now well into no-man's-land with the French frontier only a short distance ahead.

We came to a second road and, turning a bend, came on another gate, this one guarded by a sentry—but the sentry wore khaki and above his head floated the tricolor of France. We had done it. It was 13 October.

Georges was so emotionally affected that he marched forward and in full view of the sentry, snapped to attention and, bare-headed, raised his hand to his head to salute his country's flag. Then he went forward and explained who we were.

Our arrival caused quite a sensation among the ranks of the French frontier guard and the news spread like magic. With great ceremony we were escorted to a small cottage nearby where the inhabitants immediately offered us some wine, and toast after toast was drunk, first to us, then to Britain, then to the Fighting French. There were cries of *"Vive la France"* and *"A bas les Bosches"* while everyone slapped us on the back and shook their fists in the direction of the frontier.

Dear old Georges was in his element. He did not suffer from undue modesty and made us blush as he boasted of our exploits while more and more bottles of wine were opened. Johnnie and I had been greatly alarmed when he approached the frontier post with such bravado and were not at all confident of our reception. Although the relief at finding ourselves heroes coupled with the quantities of wine exhilarated us, we thought it prudent to try and stem Georges' flow of reminiscences, but it was no good. So far as he was concerned he was home with his own people and free to continue the struggle. He was no longer a fellow fugitive but our host in his homeland and nothing was too good for us.

In fact there were a number of formalities to be observed at the frontier post before we were allowed to proceed and, delayed by the celebration, it was some time before we were able to get on our way. Then, with one of the frontier guards as a guide, we set out for the nearest habitation.

News of our arrival had gone before us so that when we arrived at the little village of Pujols, there was quite a crowd gathered to greet us. Under the patronage of Georges, who took this warm reception as our right, we were introduced all round, the wine flowed again and great quantities of food appeared from nowhere. When we went to bed, utterly exhausted and not a little drunk, it was a strange feeling that we had no longer to cower in dark corners and dodge from place to place. We had, we assumed, seen the last of the Nazis and we were now quite free to move around as we wished.

The feeling persisted next day when we sat down to plan our movements. Pujols was twenty-five miles from the nearest railway station at La Réole. How to get there? Quite simple. We would hire a taxi as we still had enough francs left from what Kitty had got for us.

We ordered the taxi for ten o'clock to give us plenty of time to catch the train and we wanted to enjoy the luxury of a leisurely drive along the winding roads. The driver actually turned up at midday to catch the one o'clock train and the drive which followed was agony. As we rounded each bend on two wheels I thought bitterly that it was a sad way to end our lives after all the dangers we had successfully overcome. We did the journey in three-quarters of an hour and were deposited as quivering wrecks at the station.

We had decided to head for Marseilles as Kitty had ordained. It was the most likely port, we were told, from which we could make a break. We felt sure that with its reputation as a city where anything goes we would soon find some adventurer ready to help us on our way.

Meantime Georges had become more irrepressible than ever. Like the Ancient Mariner he regaled everyone who would listen to the story of our adventures while we became more and more apprehensive. After all *"France Libre"* was only *"France Libre"* by courtesy of the Germans and they were sure to have spies everywhere. Finally we took him aside and read him a sharp lecture about the necessity of keeping up our security. It was no use. He promised us faithfully that he would say no more but at Toulouse a midlde-aged lady and her two pretty daughters got into our carriage. For five minutes Georges ignored them while they gazed at us, obviously trying to work out our relationship. Then he could stand it no longer and was soon in full flood again. We sighed and sat back helplessly while we were plied with questions.

At Marseilles station we soon realized that matters were not to be as simple as they had been so far. There was strict control at the barriers and everybody was being asked to produce their passports and identity papers. For a time we hung around uncertainly until Georges, as bold as ever, strode up to one of the gendarmes and whispered something in his ear. Whatever it was it had the desired effect and we were quickly signalled through. The incident, however, rather upset Georges' confidence and from then on he was more easily persuaded to step warily and keep his mouth shut.

None of us knew Marseilles but Kitty had given us the

name of a man who had handled some of her people before and from whom she had suggested we should seek help. By the time we arrived, however, it was too late for us to visit him so we set about finding somewhere to eat without coupons. In this we were lucky and had a good meal. We were not so lucky, however, when it came to finding a place to lay our heads. We consulted the waiter who served us in the cafe and he recommended an hotel which turned out to be in one of the slummiest districts of a town which is far from short of slums. The hotel itself was no better than its surroundings. In all our wanderings we had come across nothing worse and we spent a miserable night in four flea-ridden beds. We were warned to be out at an early hour as the police made daily inspections of every hotel register and it would not do for us to be found there without papers.

Kitty's contact was in an office down a side-street near the American Consulate. He proved a most helpful man and quickly put us in the picture. We learnt that the position in Marseilles was very strange indeed. By virtue of the armistice conditions with Germany, and now also with Italy, British escapees in *"France Libre"* were made internees and Marseilles was the collecting centre. There were already over a hundred officers and men in the town and these, generally speaking, were accommodated in the Fort St Jean which visitors to Marseilles will remember as a gloomy building built on a bluff overlooking the old Port. Some officers, however, were allowed to live with friends outside the fortress provided they reported to the military authorities twice a week.

Thus if we had the means or the friends there was no reason why we should not live as free as other citizens provided we gave our parole not to escape—a ruling that was not very strictly enforced. The French had no objection to our escaping so long as they were not involved. If we did not give our parole or cancelled it in writing they felt they were under no further obligation to the Germans.

It was while these matters were being explained to us that I asked Kitty's contact if he had heard anything of my friend Colin Hunter. To my utmost surprise, he said that he had arrived a week or two before and that he knew him well. As a result of a telephone call we were visited ten minutes later by a young 'Frenchman' in a dark suit with black hair brushed well back.

We scarcely recognized each other, so great was the transformation in us both since June. I broke the ice by saying:

"What are you doing so far from Doullens?" A moment later we fell on each other's neck in true latin style.

Then we had a council of war. Kitty's contact told us that we would be very welcome to stay with some friends of his just outside the town but that by doing so we should be out of the centre of things and might miss any chance of getting away. Getting away from Marseilles was apparently no easy business and many of the residents in Fort St Jean had given up trying and were now resigned to spending the rest of the war there.

As a counter-proposition Colin told us that he was living in a cafe in a very poor quarter of the town with another Britisher named Gordon, who turned out to be the wounded corporal of the Buffs whom Kitty had rescued so uncomfortably in the boot of her car. It might be possible, Colin thought, for the cafe to take us in also.

This seemed sense to us, particularly as it meant being with Colin again and being able to take advantage of his few week's seniority as a Marseilles resident. Accordingly we said goodbye to our friend and set off with Colin to what was to become our new home.

If we had feared that the unexpected arrival of four

more waifs and strays would not be welcomed we could not have been more mistaken. The owner of the cafe, the Bar de la Conception, was called Lulu—not exactly an appropriate name. Lulu was a man of enormous size and strength with a craggy face which beamed friendship. He claimed to be the champion weight-lifter of France and, looking at him, we were not prepared to contradict him. He was more than a rival to Georges. He greeted us with tremendous *joie de vivre*, shaking us each vigorously by the hand to the point of almost taking our arms off. Then he introduced us to the other residents who numbered no less than eight, most of whom were relations. Lulu was not married but one of the women he introduced us to was his partner, Madame Chaix, and she in turn had a share in another cafe in Cannes which was run by her husband and which she visited periodically to check how he was getting on. Altogether a very odd arrangement but then where Lulu was involved one accepted the oddest situations as quite normal. Madame Chaix had a daughter of seventeen, Odette, who was an attractive girl and helped in the cafe, assisted by her cousin Pierette who was about the same age. Madame Chaix also had a sister who served at the confectionery counter and she had two small children under ten. Finally there was an elderly bar-tender whom we never got to know well.

Fortunately not all this gang slept in so Lulu at once suggested that Johnnie and I find some space on the first floor. Georges and Maroc he could not cope with but he very generously agreed that they should have their meals with us. Being French it would be easier for them to find other accommodation than it would be for us. Thus most days we sat down fourteen to meals before they got around to serving the paying customers.

Marseilles has a world-wide reputation as the haunt of

desperate characters who would cut your throat for the price of a meal, quite apart from the polyglot collection of prostitutes, pimps and other undesirables who haunt the dock area ready to pounce on any unwary seaman. It was near this area that Lulu ran his cafe but such was his reputation that we never had any trouble from the undesirables. Lulu was kindness itself. Gordon's leg had not really healed and he still needed hospital treatment. Like Colin he had never registered with the authorities so he was unable to obtain medical help officially. Lulu arranged it all behind the scenes. There was a big municipal hospital next door and some of the orderlies used to come into the cafe. Through them he arranged for a very pretty nurse, Juliette Rosa, to come in two or three times a day to dress his leg. Not only was there no charge but she had to risk her job by stealing the dressings and instruments required for the treatment. It was just one of the many things we had to thank Lulu for.

No sooner were we installed in the cafe than we started to make plans to escape from France. Lulu "chaired" our meetings, turning down some schemes as impractical, others as requiring too much money and putting up many suggestions of his own. At first he refused resolutely to accept any cash from our dwindling funds but was eventually persuaded to take a miserable ten francs a day—something under two shillings—for our keep.

Money now became once more our major problem. Whilst we had enough for our day-to-day needs, a considerable amount of capital was required to bribe any of the many people who were bribeable. We appealed to the American Consulate but, as in Paris, we were too late. Up until quite recently considerable sums had been paid out to would-be escapers but that had now stopped. We heard of one man who raised fifteen hundred pounds to buy a motor boat for

144

16 The author with Kitty Bonnefous at his home in Scotland in 1959.

17 (Left to right) The local military commander and the mayor of St Valéry with the author and Lt-Colonel Ian Critchley, commanding the 51st Highland Volunteers, at the celebrations on the 25th anniversary of the town's liberation.

18 The author with Madame Maille at the Crieff Games in 1971.

his break away but the money got into the hands of cut throats and not only was there no boat but not a penny was ever recovered. With Lulu to advise us we were not likely to fall into a similar trap but meantime all the Consulate would offer was an American identity card and ten or fifteen pounds with the admonition that it should be spent sparingly on our personal maintenance. After a few visits it became obvious that we could expect no help from that quarter.

One of our nagging worries during the previous weeks was that we had been unable to inform our relatives at home that we were still in the land of the living. Those who were already in prison camps had been able to inform their relatives through the Red Cross and we were very conscious that we must have been posted as missing and our next of kin would, for lack of any other news, have begun to assume that we were dead. Years later I saw the London *Times* notice announcing that I was safely behind bars in a certain German prison camp, which was almost worse for my parents as they could not contact me there. Now a new opportunity arose through the offices of a Presbyterian Minister, Donald Caskie, who was running the Marseilles Mission to Seamen. One of his special cares was to pass on the names of any British subjects he came across by simple code to the Church of Scotland in Edinburgh who in turn communicated with their families. We now approached him.

He was one of the most courageous and delightful characters I have ever met. He worked fearlessly and untiringly for anyone who came to his mission hostel. He was a West Highlander from the island of Islay but had spent most of his life on the Continent. Through this wonderful man whose book, *The Tartan Pimpernel*, later brought him deserved fame, my parents received a letter dated 21

145

October from the Scottish Church's overseas department to say that I was alive and well and able to receive letters in Marseilles. In retrospect this seems incredible but it really worked because before I finally left Marseilles I received a letter from my mother written on 26 October.

Donald Caskie had quite a large establishment in Marseilles. Besides one big room set aside as a dormitory for fifty or sixty strays, there were billiards rooms, meeting rooms and a small chapel to which Johnnie, Colin and I often repaired on a Sunday.

We went to the mission as often as we could as this was the one place where we could meet friends, but as unregistered escapees we had to be careful as the place was naturally kept under constant surveillance. It was there that I met a Quartermaster Sergeant of my own Regiment and learned with some pride that there were no less than eighteen other Cameron Highlanders who had made it this far and were now waiting for their chance to move on further.

There were two escape stories which I heard. One concerns a group of Jocks from an Argyll battalion who were all Gaelic speakers. They were arrested by the Germans and held for the night. Whilst they were under arrest and during their interrogation next morning they spoke nothing but Gaelic. This so bewildered the Germans that they got out a map and asked them to point out where they came from. One of them selected a point in the far north of Russia and the others solemnly nodded their agreement. This so confused their captors that they let them go.

The other story concerns my own battalion. An N.C.O. was trying to get out of Northern France with a young private soldier from our Regiment but could not cross over any of the bridges over the Somme as they were closely guarded. The N.C.O. was intelligent and quick-witted but his companion was reserved and dour. They managed to

146

bribe a boatman to row them over the river but when they reached the rendezvous they found the boat there but no boatman. They waited for some time and then decided to row themselves across. They were in mid stream when they were hailed by two German officers from the bank they had just left. The N.C.O. was all for ignoring the summons but the boy, taking command of the situation, put back to shore to find that the officers only wanted a lift. They were duly taken over but as they nodded their thanks and made to walk off the young boy stuck out his hand and demanded a tip. The Germans paid up two francs each!

Later we met an English Captain who had also been in the barracks at Tournai. After some questioning we discovered that he was the officer who had escaped with the Doctor just before us and who, we had been told by that wretched sergeant major, had been machine-gunned. As we suspected at the time it had been a tissue of lies and now we had the evidence.

Marseilles was a small world for the British in those days. Many and ingenious were the plans being made all around us for escape. After the failure of the motor boat plan which was intended to take a large number of escapees, the serious ones had broken up into groups of threes and fours and each had their own idea of how to get away. One or two groups favoured crossing the Pyrénées into Spain. Others considered trying to stow away in ships bound for Algeria and Tunisia but these particular hopes were dashed by the arrival of two men from Oran who had come to Marseilles in the belief that it was easier to escape from there. One man I met planned to cross the Atlantic to Martinique and several people put their faith in the idea of jumping from a boat passing the Straits of Gibraltar and swimming ashore.

I did not favour any of these schemes, regarding them

147

as likely to take me from the frying pan into the fire, but I did toy with the idea of joining the French Foreign Legion with a view to being sent to Casablanca, where it was known that soldiers could get demobilized. However, one of our companions tried this and was detected at the outset because he was carrying so much money in his belt to buy his discharge that it was obvious he was no potential Legionnaire —the last resort of the poverty stricken.

Spain was the unknown quantity. If one was lucky with one's contacts it might have been possible to succeed—and many did—but there were stories of some who had crossed the Pyrénées being sent back to the Germans in occupied France. There were alliance talks going on between Spain's Suñer, Italy's Ciano and Germany's Ribbentrop at this time and the body of public opinion in Spain was against us. A sea journey seemed the only answer—but where to?

We began to see less and less of Georges. He still came to the cafe for his meals but he was wrapped up in his own schemes for escape. He was quite ready to buy or steal a boat and sail for Gibraltar but he was not prepared to stow away on a French ship. It would have been too much for his sense of honour to France if he had been discovered and sent back with ignominy. Poor Georges! In the end he managed to raise the considerable sum of five thousand francs for the purchase of a boat but, like the fifteen hundred pounds, it fell into the hands of the crooks and he was stranded without any hope of being able to raise such a large sum again. The last I heard of him until well after the war was that he was considering compromising his principles and going to Algiers, which in 1940 was still Vichy controlled.

One of the oddest characters we met at Lulu's was a fat, cheery, little French detective called Ballygand who had an

Irish mother and spoke English perfectly. He was paid to keep an eye and report on the unregistered British but he did not take his job very seriously and spent much of his time coffee-housing with us. He did half-heartedly suggest to Johnnie and me that we should give our parole but, when we showed no enthusiasm, he dropped the matter.

Ballygand would not actively help us escape but he joined enthusiastically in advising us if any of our many plans was feasible. He also proved to be the British soldier's friend. If any of them were caught out in a misdemeanour like getting drunk he covered up for them or saw that they got off lightly. Twice he stopped us from embarking on schemes which would have had no chance of success and gradually we came to trust him—so much so that we agreed to register at the Fort provided we did not have to live there.

"After all," he told us, "what can you lose? You only have to cancel your parole in writing, give it to a friend to hand in and clear off." It was a farcical state of affairs.

Every day we heard news of fresh attempts at escape. Often we bade "Goodbye and God Speed" to a friend—for most of them came to Lulu's cafe—only to greet them with "Good-day" the following morning. Nine out of ten plots failed. It was not encouraging.

The days passed slowly. Every morning we had an escape conference, drawing on the experience of anyone we could, but by lunch time we were left with nothing to do. Mostly we went to the films. There were a surprising number of English films showing which had been translated into the French. *Elle et Lui* for example was rather better than the English original *Love Affair*. We even saw *Gunga Din* and risked a cheer as the Black Watch came on the screen playing their Regimental March. There were a lot of newsreel cinemas showing vitriolic anti-British propaganda. It was gratifying to hear the French audiences shouting in derision as some of the more obviously slanted incidents were shown. Maurice Chevalier was in Marseilles one day and I saw him holding court in a cafe. Unfortunately I did not have the courage to go up and speak to him.

One of the advantages of declaring ourselves at Fort St Jean was that we were issued with ration cards, which were not normally issued as the residents in the Fort were fed free but, living outside in the cafe, it was allowed. It was some assistance to Lulu as food was in short supply. The South of France is primarily a wine growing area and there is very little locally reared beef. Soon horse was being advertised as a delicacy and before long even that was almost unobtainable. How Lulu managed to feed us so well has always remained a mystery to me.

We had generally been given to believe when we were in the north of France that the southern French, not having suffered the indignities of German occupation, were far more anti-British than their northern neighbours. This in fact was not true. Most were fervent de Gaulle supporters and many regarded Churchill as the saviour of Europe. British communiques were often printed in the papers alongside the German ones for censorship was far less strict than it was in the north. I was in a crowded bar one evening when Churchill made his famous speech in French to the French appealing to them to be patient and have courage. At the words *"C'est moi Churchill qui vous parle"* in a forthright British accent everyone cheered or cried with emotion.

The Germans made every effort to counter the pro-British feeling. On one occasion they adopted a clever ruse. They scattered leaflets all over the town saying that they had been dropped from British aircraft. The leaflets were very British in character and ended with the words,

"Take note, Frenchmen, the flag of France will fly over your country again in ninety days!" Of course the promise was impossible of fulfilment and the Germans hoped that the French would take this as a breach of faith. Within hours British Intelligence had issued a statement over the Free French network denying authorship of the leaflet and the Germans were thoroughly discredited.

Everything, however, did not go our way. Towards the end of September, before we arrived, the British had bombed Marseilles in mistake for another target and the incident, not unnaturally, caused a lot of ill-feeling. The bombs fell in the slum area and caused much damage. For some weeks afterwards there was harsh criticism of the British but it did not lessen the general hatred for Marshal Pétain's henchman, Laval!

About this time I contracted the extremely painful skin disease which the French called *La Gale*, which is the same as scabies and not to be boasted about. I was in agony. Juliette, Gordon's pretty nurse, promised to take me under her wing but the cure was almost worse than the disease. With no regard for my modesty she made me take off all my clothes and massaged me from head to foot with sulphur ointment which stung like a thousand wasps. I soon forgot my blushes and ground my teeth in pain as the treatment proceeded. After a few days of this the disease showed signs of improvement and Juliette decreed another and even more agonising course. This time I had to buy a liquid preparation from the chemist which was predominantly sulphur but seemed to me more like undiluted acid. To prepare for the application I had to take as hot a bath as I could. None of the poor houses we knew had such luxuries as a bath so she smuggled me into the hospital. I cannot adequately describe the agony I now went through. To get the liquid well into the pores she dabbed it on with a bristly artist's brush.

With my flesh red and raw from the hot bath it was torture and I frequently leapt from my seat and danced round the room, all dignity gone to the winds. Of course Johnnie and the others thought all this highly amusing and begged to be allowed to come and watch but this was sternly forbidden by Juliette.

Finally I had a course of more sulphur baths, this time in the public bath house. Juliette insisted on buying only one ticket and firmly locked us both into the cubicle. What the attendant thought I do not know. Perhaps simply *"Vive le sport"*. Anyway I was temporarily cured.

Johnnie and I made a lot of friends among the British who were wandering around Marseilles. There was Pat, a gunner who had been with the 51st Highland Division; Alastair, an Argyll with a game leg who had somehow managed to get out of Occupied France in spite of it. There was also an American, Bill, who had been with the American Volunteer Red Cross, and Georges, a Belgian Jew with an English wife living near Liverpool.

Georges spoke several languages fluently which enabled him to contact escape groups set up by other occupied countries and it was through him that I got in touch with a Czech organization. They worked very hard indeed for all the Allies in addition to their own nationals. They had an unofficial Consular office near the old port which was always crowded with applicants of one sort or another. It was through them that I got my first chance to escape from Marseilles.

Johnnie and I met our Czech friends early in November and from then on we more or less sat on their doorstep. One day the head of the organization called us into a private room and told us that an opportunity had occurred to get four men away. He had three Czechs who must take priority and he could offer the fourth place to one of us. The destination was Beirut. Johnnie and I talked it over and he generously gave up his claims to me on the ground that I already knew the area and would have a better chance of getting through.

There was one snag. The boat was leaving in two days and the bribery fee was eight thousand francs—about forty pounds—an amount which was obviously far beyond my means. Urgent discussions took place on how the money might be raised and Colin came up with a possible solution. Earlier he had stayed a few days in the country with Kitty's friend and he, a Monsieur Laupe, had told him that if there was ever a serious proposition which required money, Colin should apply to him. Colin himself was quite confident that he would get repatriated on account of his wound and offered to try and raise the money for me. The next morning he went to the man's office and returned in under an hour with the francs. It was an act of great generosity.

My excitement was now at fever pitch. I immediately went to see the Czechs and handed over the cash. They were past masters at dealing with the underworld and assured me that the cash would be held by them until all four of us were on our way and there could be no chance of betrayal. I was told to report the following evening to a certain cafe. I spent the day doing the rounds and saying goodbye to my friends. While it was quite a wrench to be leaving them behind they were all delighted for my sake. They were deeply involved with their own plans and it had just so happened that my number had come up first.

I duly reported at the appointed place and met my three voyage companions. Johnnie came with me and as he finally said goodbye, he laughingly remarked, "No doubt you will be back tomorrow morning!"

The next two hours were a real cloak and dagger drama. On reaching the port we were led into a small sailor's bar near the main gates to the dock and told to sit quietly in a corner. Our guide left us and returned after twenty minutes with a sailor who issued each of us with a yellow identity card. Ten minutes later we were standing in a queue waiting to pass a check point into the docks, which were guarded by two gendarmes. I was surprised that we had not been given sailor's clothes but I soon saw that many of the people in the queue ahead of us were wearing civilian suits. Although the Germans, and now the Italians, had no jurisdiction in Free France they controlled the ports so there was not the same freedom of movement as in the town itself. However, when it came to our turn we passed through the dock gates without the slightest trouble.

We made our way past some sheds and up a gang plank on to the boat. The deck was deserted and we had no difficulty in slipping down to the crew's quarters where we were shown into a tiny cabin and told to keep absolutely quiet. It was obvious that we were in for a frightful journey. There was hardly room for the four of us to sit down. Smoking was strictly forbidden and the porthole was to be kept firmly closed during the voyage. Five days and nights in these conditions was going to try us to the limit.

I was just getting reconciled to our situation when the cabin door opened again and the sailor who had been our guide beckoned to us to come out. A few minutes later we were again ashore and our Czech friend met us at the gates. He explained that the sailor had wanted half the money in advance and he had refused to pay it. He had little doubt that a double-cross was intended and that we should be handed over to the authorities for the sake of the reward. We were back to square one.

It was a very dejected character who presented himself back at Lulu's that night. Nobody was surprised to see me. "You will make three more attempts before you finally get away," grinned Lulu and I was accepted back as if I had never left. The only difference was that I had given up my parole but this was the least of my worries.

Shortly after this Colin was called before the medical board with the aim of being passed unfit so that he could be repatriated. The American Consulate had persuaded the Vichy authorities to allow seriously wounded Britishers to be exchanged and Colin was among a party of some thirty officers and men whose cases were up for consideration.

We went with him to the hospital and he later gave us a highly amusing account of how he had got on. There were three members of the examining board. One represented the French authorities, another the Americans and a third, a Swede, represented the Axis. The American representative was the first to examine Colin and, with a broad wink, passed him as unfit. Then came the turn of the Frenchman who sent him to an eye specialist for an opinion. The eye specialist examined Colin carefully and soon found out that he was a fraud. After telling him that there was really nothing wrong with him he said, "I suppose you want to be passed unfit. It's all the same to me. Here you are," and gave him an adverse report. After this the Swede, who had the reputation of turning everyone down, could do nothing. It was two against one.

Alas this did not mean Colin's immediate repatriation. First the papers had to be sent to Vichy, then to the German authorities in Paris and they retained the right to ask for a re-examination. By the time I finally came to leave Colin was still there, but his day of release came eventually.

Chapter 8

I was now in the depth of depression. It seemed to me that I had had my golden opportunity and it had been missed. Although I still had my eight thousand francs, the underworld was not to be trusted and I despaired of finding an honest man in Marseilles. So I was once more back to the eternal round of the cafes, of listening to other people's escape plans and of the dreadful boredom of the whole situation.

Then one day I met a very excited Pat and Bill. They had heard of a new escape scheme which, they said, was almost certain of success. At first I listened with enthusiasm but soon my heart sank. The destination was again Beirut, the general duties were the same as before and when I heard the sum required—eight thousand francs—I felt sure that they were on to the same lot as previously. But such was my desperation that I agreed to go along with them and enquire more deeply into it.

This plan also involved a group of four people. Pat and Bill were to be two if they could raise the money. I was to be a third and a French business man named Benjamin Slor was to be the fourth. In the end Pat and Bill could not find the cash so like the little nigger boys we were down to two.

I met Ben the next day and took to him immediately. He was thirty-eight, the son of a French doctor who had practised in Morocco. Ben had spent most of his life in

Paris where, at the outbreak of the war, he had been the chief engineer of an engineering firm whose chairman he was to become later. When France fell he had at once decided that his duty lay as a member of the Free French Forces, which was a courageous decision for someone of his age and station in life. Ben was small in height and no chicken like me. However, what he lacked in youth and physique he made up in shrewdness and determination. He left all his possessions with his wife and daughter in Paris and set out to try and escape to the Allies via Marseilles, taking only sufficient money for the journey. Indeed he had the best money of all—varied currencies and some gold coins—which were hidden sewn into his clothes. He had just the right mixture of characteristics suited for the enterprise on which we were about to embark. His excitable nature and patriotism was matched with much caution and cunning.

Next I met the contact man for the operation, who turned out to be a thoroughly repulsive character called Victor. He was immensely fat with shifty little pig eyes who filled me with instant foreboding. He claimed to be the cousin of a sailor on one of the liners who was prepared to take the risk of smuggling us aboard. Victor was nothing more than the worst sort of tout and Ben, who was also at the meeting, could see that I completely distrusted him.

"Don't worry about him," he said. "I know the type. Just leave him to me." Such was Ben's personality that I felt quite sure if it came to a balance of wits the scales would fall in our favour.

Again there was no time to lose. The liner, the *Mariette Pasha* of the Messagerie Maritimes, was due to sail in two days' time. The plan was for us both to go aboard early on the morning of departure with Victor's cousin, disguised as dock workers and hide up until she sailed at midday. Ben would have none of this. He insisted that he should go on board the day before without me to have time to look around and that he and Victor's cousin would then come off to fetch me after dark if all was well.

Ben prevailed and left for the ship and I again went the rounds of saying goodbye to everyone. It was particularly difficult to part from Juliette. We had grown very fond of one another and she was miserable at the prospect of my leaving. She mistrusted all the arrangements and felt sure that I was going to be cheated. My clothes were now in rags and she volunteered to get me some new ones for the journey. Pretending that they were for the French wounded, she managed to collect two shirts for me and a new pair of trousers and even gave me her attache case to carry them in.

A little before 7 pm I left to keep my cafe rendezvous with Ben, Victor and Victor's cousin. I entered the cafe to see Ben sitting in a corner having a verbal battle with Victor, but no sailor. Quite obviously something had gone very wrong. Pouring me a brandy and with much gesticulation, he explained the situation.

He had got aboard quite satisfactorily to discover that Victor's cousin, who was the ship's carpenter, insisted on half the passage money in advance. It appeared that he was no different from the rest and Ben, quite rightly, refused to part with a sou. There had followed a heated argument which had ended with Ben walking off the ship alone. However, the door was still open for reconciliation, Ben having agreed to meet the sailor at our rendezvous ashore for a further discussion.

Victor, most indignant that his cousin had been distrusted, but fearing that he was going to lose his commission on the deal, had calmed Ben down and persuaded him to re-enter negotiations. It had been agreed that the carpenter should come ashore to see if anything could be renegotiated and the meeting was scheduled for 8 pm.

When by 8.30 the man had not shown up, Victor became agitated. Ben and I had just decided to give up the whole affair and leave when two sailors rolled into the cafe, roaring drunk. One of them was the carpenter and the other one of his shipmates. This was a pretty state of affairs. Drink is the worst enemy of security and this truth was soon impressed on us as the two men started to discuss our departure at the top of their voices. Victor, now more than ever desperate at the thought of his disappearing commission, exerted his powers of arbitration to the full. He half took our side, shouting at them to behave but at the same time tried to persuade us that they were not as drunk as they seemed. We were, however, past the point of no return. We were not going to trust our sixteen thousand francs to a couple of drunken sailors.

In the end a compromise was reached. We would give them one more chance. As the boat was not sailing until noon the following day we arranged as a last resort to meet at six the next morning, while it was still dark, to see how matters stood. I did not have the heart to go back to Lulu's so I spent that night with Bill and Pat in their hotel. Good friends that they were they did everything they could to comfort Ben and me despite their disappointment at not coming with us.

The following morning we kept our appointment on the dot but this time neither Victor nor the sailors turned up. We waited for two hours in despair. As it might be months before such an opportunity came again and we could stand the waiting no longer, we decided that we would go to the dock ourselves to see the lie of the land. Ben, having already been aboard, knew the geography. Fortunately there were a lot of stevedores passing through the gate and, by mingling with them, we passed the gendarmes without trouble. By now we were both experienced dock-gate passers.

Once on board ship we went straight to the carpenter's cabin and sat down and waited for him. Ten minutes later he walked in and almost fell over with surprise. Sober, he turned out to be a chicken-hearted creature. He told us that he had decided not to take the risk and that he had purposely not kept the rendezvous. So far as he was concerned the deal was off.

Our position was now, however, much stronger. We were already aboard and half the danger was over. We told him that we would not move until he brought his companion of the night before to talk the matter over with us. This man, Noel Galetti by name, proved to be of altogether different fibre. He was quite prepared to relieve his friend both of the responsibility and the money and look after us during the voyage. He was a tough Corsican with no scruples whatsoever, but he did not lack courage.

A snag now arose because Galetti, being an ordinary member of the crew, shared his sleeping quarters with twenty others and he had no place to hide us. The carpenter, being cut out of the deal, was no longer prepared to let us use his cabin but he was persuaded to let us stay there until after the ship sailed. In return he received a thousand francs hush money. It gave us considerable satisfaction to know that, under these new arrangements, the deplorable Victor would also lose his commission.

Galetti, having once undertaken responsibility for us, proved most conscientious. He spent the time before we sailed rushing round the ship trying to find somewhere to hide us and came back to us frequently to report progress. We were moved to a crew mess room as a temporary expedient and there he brought us some food and sour wine, telling us to eat as much as we could because he could not guarantee when we should get our next meal.

The ship sailed exactly on time and it was with much exhilaration that we heard the engines start and felt the motion as we put to sea. Soon we were moved across to the ship's sickbay, which was positioned in the stern. There we were locked into a small cabin, better than the one on the previous ship but still very cramped. Again we were instructed not to open the porthole except for a couple of hours at night.

Now there started a marathon of endurance. To begin with we were both seasick, which was perhaps just as well as we got no food for the next thirty-six hours and were only let out at rare intervals to go to the lavatory. A medical orderly had been enlisted to look after us but he was so terrified of his charge that he seldom came near us. Galetti only came down once and then we fired so many questions at him that he quickly left.

We spent much of the time discussing what we should do if we were torpedoed by a British ship. At times, even though there was the risk of being drowned, it seemed to us preferable to being cramped in our little black hole of Calcutta. We should no doubt have realized that a Vichy passenger ship would have a free passage from both sides. Only once did we hear an aeroplane and peering out of the porthole were able to see that it was a British flying boat looking us over.

After some thirty-six hours we entered calmer water and heard the engines stop and felt the boat slowly come to a halt. A moment later Galetti shot into our cabin and urged us to follow him. He led us into the bowels of the ship explaining that we were in the straits of Messina and that the Italian police were coming aboard on a routine inspection. It crossed our minds that quite a few people knew

161

we were on board and that we might be given away, but the crisis passed and after an hour we were on our way once more, back in our quarters.

We almost welcomed this exciting interlude as a break from the five days and nights we spent on that voyage. At last, soon after dawn on the morning of 21 November, we heard the engines slow once more and, peering out, could just make out land ahead. Half an hour later we were alongside.

After our long imprisonment we looked forward to an early release, but Galetti decided that it was not safe for me to go ashore till darkness. Meantime I had been moved down to the crew's quarters and given a bunk to lie on. I spent a miserable day with nothing to eat or drink, bathed in perspiration and kept busy picking the cockroaches off the mattress. I suppose the crew were used to these conditions but I found them ghastly. It had been decided that Ben should go ashore with Galetti soon after docking to reconnoitre and seek out the British Consul. I watched through the porthole as the two of them walked brazenly off the boat and set off up the quay. Then there was nothing to do but wait. I passed twelve hours of sheer agony while my imagination worked overtime. I pictured Ben being arrested and myself abandoned in Beirut or even being carried back to Marseilles. My heart stopped pounding when around six in the evening Galetti came back for me. French sailors going ashore wore a mixture of a uniform coat and civilian hat and trousers. He took a jacket from a nearby bunk for me and, borrowing a pass from one of his mates, he led me up the companionway and on to the gangplank. It was absurdly easy. We strolled off the boat without anyone taking the slightest notice and set off to join Ben who was waiting for us in a nearby cafe. "He has good news for you," Galetti told me. Personally I was so hungry by this time that news could wait. I had not eaten for thirty-six hours.

We found Ben in the far corner of the biggest cafe in the square and in front of him was a large bottle of wine. Without more ado I ordered one of the most enormous meals of my life, but being so hungry I cannot remember what I ate. Then came the final settlement with Galetti. Before we paid him we discussed whether he might not be prepared to rescue some more of our comrades in the same way. He may have been a rogue but he was also brave and he readily agreed. I think I managed to convince him that the British authorities would pay him for anyone he delivered. Whether our arrangements came to anything or not I have never found out but I do know that our ship was the last one to get a safe conduct.

The money having been passed over we were all now in high spirits and the best of friends. Ben said that he understood that we could move about Beirut as freely as we wished. We did not realize the risks and in our ignorance we readily fell in with Galetti when he suggested that he show us the town. By this time he was Noel and we were Ben and Derek.

Ben and I took a taxi and called on the British Consulate, to find that the place was deserted and there was only an Arab caretaker outside the house. We learned that the Consulate staff had moved to Aleih in the mountains on the road to Damascus. The Arab seemed quite mystified when we asked him to confirm that we could move around the city freely. He could see no reason why not but he was just an Arab watchman. Why should he have known the political implications of the British in Syria? We were very naive and gullible.

We returned to Noel ready for anything and at once started on a tour of all the lowest night spots to be found.

Wherever we went Noel was greeted with delight by bar-maids, waitresses and ladies of the town. Everywhere he was known to everybody. There was no blackout. The cafes were brightly lit and crowded with people. There was certainly no war on so far as Beirut was concerned.

By two in the morning we were on our knees with tired-ness and begged Noel to call a halt and find us somewhere to sleep. He took us to one of the sleaziest buildings I have ever seen and introduced us to two flea-bitten looking Arabs sitting at a table in front of the "hotel" register. They quoted a price which seemed to us very cheap, but Noel was outraged, telling them that we were only a couple of poor sailors. Eventually the price was cut in half and we rolled into bed in what we were later to learn was a well-known sailor's brothel. Our night fortunately was undisturbed. Noel had proved a man of his word and quite a character. We said goodbye to him with real regret—something we would never have imagined when we first set eyes on him in Marseilles.

Ben refrained from discussing our affairs in front of Noel but now that we were alone in the bedroom he told me that he had contacted a girl whose address he had been given in Marseilles. She too had told him that we were in no danger in Beirut and could move about openly. Up to this point we were full of confidence and sallied forth next morning, leaving our two meagre suitcases in the hotel, to hire a taxi to drive the fifteen miles into the hills to Aleih. There were a Frenchman and his wife also going to the British Consulate so we agreed to share a cab and happily chatted of our experiences all the way. I was almost as bad as old Georges had been and I later turned cold when I knew of the risks we had run.

We got the true facts when Ben and I were shown in to see the Vice-Consul. His first words were, "How on earth

164

did you get here without being stopped?" followed by, "My problem now is how the hell to get you out again." It was not the warm welcome I was expecting and my stock with Ben sank.

Apparently ever since the capitulation of France and the installation of the Vichy régime pro-British officials had been removed and one of the first measures had been to order our Consulate out of Beirut. The French were keeping the closest watch on our consulate staff and the building was under day and night surveillance. It was sheer luck that we had missed the guard on our arrival but, as the Vice-Consul explained miserably, we would almost certainly not be so lucky on departure and we had to depart soon.

The thought that we could still be arrested and interned was deeply distressing. We had been so elated the previous night thinking that all our troubles were over. Ben's situation was, if anything, worse than mine. I was, at least, able to enlist the aid of my own countrymen. He was nobody's child and an embarrassment to them. If I had not pointed out most forcibly how much he had helped me, they would have washed their hands of him.

After my interview with the Vice-Consul I was taken in to see the Consul-General. He agreed to take Ben under his wing providing I would vouch for him when and if we reached British territory. The Consul-General thought it likely that by our conduct we had already raised suspicions and urged that we be doubly careful. I would be lodged until further notice with a retired Consular official, but Ben would have to fend for himself with money which they would provide.

The time came for us to run the gauntlet to get out of the Embassy and back to Beirut. The Vice-Consul walked down the stairs and out of the front door jabbering away in French. As we feared, a French detective immediately came across to us to ask for our identity cards. Ignoring the request, the Vice-Consul engaged him in rapid conversation, mostly about the weather, while Ben and I dodged round the back of the taxi, which was mercifully still waiting for us. Our friend went on crying "*Il fait beau temps*" to keep the detective occupied and a moment later we were racing down the hill back to the city.

The French couple who had come up with us were already seated in the car waiting for us. It was essential that we should get back to Beirut before the police posts in between could be alerted. No time was wasted on that journey as we rocked round corners at full speed. We stopped the driver about a mile short of the Grande Place, where we paid our dues and got out and walked.

Over lunch Ben and I made a few last-minute arrangements. He had a contact who would provide him with somewhere to lie up and I was to meet a guide who was to take me to my new temporary home. I was sorry to leave him and felt I was rather letting him down. I consoled myself with the thought that I would soon be in a position to help him, so, after getting his address, we parted company.

I arrived at my appointed rendezvous to see someone who must clearly be waiting for me busy studying a shop window. Without any sign of recognition he moved off rapidly with me following close behind in true James Bond style. We walked for about ten minutes before turning into a small gate and a moment later I was shaking hands with my volunteer host.

This man was kindness itself and it was a great treat to be in a civilized house after slumming it for so many weeks. In my relief I was bubbling over with excitement, my depression momentarily forgotten. I told him my whole story and when I had finished he said:

"I know an Arab in the mountains who is a village headman or Muktar who has great influence and I am sure that he can help you by providing a guide who will take you over the mountains to the Palestinian frontier."

I explained to him that the Consul-General was planning that I should stay with him for some time. The poor chap was horrified.

"Much as I would like to have you, it is impossible," he told me. "What the Consul does not realize is that I am as much watched as he is or any of his assistants. If you were to go into the street now, you would find a small yellow car parked against the pavement a few hundred yards away. It is owned by a detective who stays there all day and only goes away after dark." It was clear that something would have to be done as soon as possible. My host told me that he had some people coming in for drinks that evening and that he would enlist their help.

The guests turned up in quick succession. The first was a lady secretary from the American Legation, the second the manager of the Syrian branch of Socony Vacuum and the third a native of Jersey who had had a small business in Beirut for a number of years. They were all astonished when they learned that I was an escaping Britisher and at once all three offered to help.

It was decided that it was too dangerous for me to stay even one night in the house and that the man from Jersey, David Murphy, should take me over and collect Ben in the morning. The following day the Socony man, Bill Rinder, was to send his car for us and provide us with food for the long drive into the mountains. Meantime my host was to provide us with a letter of introduction to his Muktar friend.

Accordingly, soon after dark David and I left the house and travelled by tram to his home. He had a Greek wife and they were both over sixty. We sat far into the night discussing the position and planning the future of any other escapees who might follow in my footsteps. David was a great enthusiast and offered to be the intermediary between Noel Galetti and the British and guarantee the money.

The car was due at eleven the next day and in the morning David had to go for our bags, collect Ben and buy some food. He had an uneasy time at the hotel. The owners told him that the police had been in to check the register and discovering that our bags were still there intended to call back. His visit came just before the police. None the less he accomplished all his tasks and was back with Ben with half an hour to spare.

Chapter 9

The Socony Vacuum car turned out to be a big American
Nash and arrived at the door dead on time. The driver had
been told nothing about us other than that we were to be
driven to a certain village in the mountains and handed over
to the Muktar. He was a well-educated Arab who spoke
English and French perfectly. It was quite obvious that he
knew something was afoot but he asked no questions. We
spun him some yarn about how we had come over the
frontier from Iraq and wanted to avoid precious time going
through the French customs. It was a story which would not
have deceived a child but he went along with it happily
and proved a most cheerful companion.

The driver's instructions were to avoid the main roads
out of Beirut. Accordingly we twisted and turned our way
through the suburbs until we came out on the Haifa coast
road clear of the town. We had been told that there were
control posts only on the main roads, so after travelling
five or six miles, he turned left on to a second class road
and started climbing. In fact our information was wrong
and we soon passed a gendarme standing outside a police
post. Fortunately he took no notice but I was later to learn
that when the car returned it was stopped and the driver
was asked what had happened to his two passengers. He
denied having had anyone with him saying the gendarme
must have mistaken the car and nothing more was said. Our
luck was holding.

We reached the village between two and three in the afternoon. It was a remote spot and our big car attracted a great deal of attention. We had to wait while a messenger was sent to the fields to find the Muktar. He turned out to be a most interesting character. Taking us to his house he ordered tea and fruit and talked to us in fluent English. He told us that there was a great deal of discontent amongst the Lebanese with their Vichy French masters and that the general feeling was in favour of the Free French and British taking over. They were suffering great privation due to the blockade and the knowledge that their brothers in Palestine had everything they wanted caused much ill-feeling. His influence extended for many miles around and he assured us that his people would rise to a man if the Allies came to their rescue.

When we discussed the journey ahead he warned us that only a certain distance could be covered by car and the rest of the way was hard going on foot. We were a little worried by this as we only had thin town shoes, unsuitable for rough ground, and neither of us was marching fit. However with freedom just round the corner these were minor considerations and we waited anxiously for our guide.

About four o'clock Mustapha, a swarthy-looking ruffian, who we felt would cut our throats at the first opportunity, arrived. The Muktar assured us that he was the soul of loyalty and that we could trust him implicitly. We bade our friend goodbye and set off with Mustapha in front with the driver on the last stage of our journey.

We took a rough winding road south and just before passing through a second village Mustapha indicated that it would be safer if Ben and I were to get out and make a detour on foot. We were getting to the boundaries of the Muktar's influence. We walked for about a mile but the rough going made us quite exhausted and we worried even more about the trials ahead. It was just as well that we had gone on foot, however, as the car was stopped and the driver's papers examined.

By five o'clock it started to get dark and we had to switch on our lights. Mustapha was not too happy about this. A car was unusual enough in this area without advertising our presence. Before we reached the next village he called a halt and said that the time had come for us to take to our feet.

We had no idea how far we were going to have to walk but Mustapha told us that we should reach the frontier at six the next morning, so we estimated that it could not be more than ten to fifteen miles. How wrong we were.

We skirted the village and were challenged by a Lebanese but were allowed to pass when Mustapha explained that we were visiting friends in the next village. The improbability of two lounge-suited Europeans carrying suitcases visiting a remote Arab village at that time of night was obvious, but who were we to argue.

On and on we walked, slipping and stumbling over the rough ground. Mustapha seemed to glide over the ground and was always drawing farther and farther ahead. Then he would stop and wait impatiently for us to catch up. It was soon obvious that he might have been able to reach the frontier that night but we certainly would not.

After four hours I was feeling the strain and poor Ben was in even worse shape. At this point we came to the top of a huge ravine and we could hear water rushing far below. Mustapha warned us that the crossing might be guarded and to walk very quietly. There was some sort of pathway down but we quickly lost it and kept sprawling over in the scrub. In the dark and in our state of fatigue it was torture. At almost every step, it seemed, we tripped over a loose stone which went crashing to the bottom. There was no guard post which was just as well.

When we finally reached the water Ben and I threw ourselves face downwards, splashing it over our heads and drinking deeply in spite of Mustapha's horrified warnings. Then we went on strike. Mustapha was impatient to push on but we were quite unable to move another step until we had had a rest. We lay down feeling that we would never get up again. While we rested he went on a reconnaissance and reported that the way was clear.

It was all we could do to get up the other side of the ravine and then the dreadful plod continued. We had been doing about two and a half miles an hour. Now we were only making half that speed. By 3 am we could go no further. Ben's feet were in ribbons from blisters and I was so exhausted I could not move another step. At first Mustapha tried to haul us along by grabbing our hands but it was no use. He realized that we had had as much as we could take and set about looking for somewhere for us to lie up until the following night.

He led us to some mud huts silhouetted against the sky line. Entering the biggest one, we lay down and were at once asleep. When we woke it was long after daylight. We took stock of our unusual surroundings and found that we were in a stonebuilt croft which was bare except for a pile of rugs and clothing in the far corner. Suddenly to our amazement the rugs began to move and we found that we were not the only living things in the place. We were even more amazed when a human face appeared and a voice addressed us in fluent English.

"I am Mustapha's cousin," it said. "My name is Ahmed. Welcome to my olive mill."

Seeing our astonishment, he explained:

"I speak your language because I was in Canada for ten

years as a young man. Now I am old, over seventy, and I have come back to spend my last years in my own country."

It seemed to us extraordinary that someone who had once enjoyed the standard of living of the West could return to such squalor, but he proved a kindly man and told us that we would be quite safe in his house. He supplied us with unleavened bread and sour milk throughout the day while we nursed our feet and prepared ourselves for the renewal of the ordeal that night.

Ahmed had a long and earnest discussion with Mustapha and then told us that he considered the route we were taking was far too arduous in view of our condition and that Mustapha would go and fetch a new guide for us who knew an easier path. This time the estimate of the time required for the rest of the journey was three hours. Mentally we doubled this and were proved to be right.

The day's rest had done us a great deal of good and we set out at nightfall with Ali, our new guide, in quite good spirits. To our delight, instead of climbing farther, we descended to a grass strip on level ground. Mustapha, although his services were not really required, came with us so that he would be able to report to his Muktar that we had successfully completed the journey. Ali walked in front and Mustapha brought up the rear. In spite of the easier going progress was slow and after a short time Ben's feet started to play him up again. After frequent stops and when it was nearly midnight we climbed to the top of a rise and, looking over the top, saw the lights of a village burning below us. "Palestine!" whispered Ali.

We were so excited that, if Mustapha and Ali had not restrained us, we would have rushed forward. They warned us that the most dangerous part of the journey had begun and that the frontier was closely guarded by both sides.

We started to creep forward over the last half mile, like

scouts on patrol, moving only a few yards at a time. We were practically in the village and about to stand up and declare ourselves when two Verey lights went up on our right and several shots were fired. They were not aimed at us but they told us what we wanted to know—where the nearest post was. We therefore turned to the left off the skyline, down a slope and over a stream. The stream was the frontier and we were in Palestine. After five and a half months I was free! It was 20 November.

Passing through an orange grove, we came to a tarmac road leading into the main street of the village. I do not know what we expected in the way of a greeting but whatever it was we certainly did not get it! The street lights burned brightly but there was not a soul about. Thinking of all the villages we had dodged in the course of our escape it was comical to think that now that we wanted to be recognized we could not raise a soul. We hammered at the door of a hostel but without the slightest reaction. Next we tried one or two of the more important looking houses but with the same result. We were anxious to establish that there was no mistake and that we really were in Palestine. I had heard of escapees in Europe in the Great War failing at the last moment through mistaking the Dutch–German frontier and we certainly did not want that to happen to us.

Eventually we managed to get someone to come to a door only to tell us to go away. The four of us returned to the hostel and sat down on its steps to wait for morning. Ben and I burst out laughing so ridiculous was the situation.

We had hardly sat down, however, when we heard the sound of marching feet. A moment later a British soldier appeared out of the gloom doing his rounds, his rifle slung over his shoulder, and we knew we were safe. The sight of

174

a British Tommy in uniform after so many months of viewing the enemy was altogether too much for me. With a shout of joy I rushed into the roadway and threw my arms round his neck!

His reaction was understandable. He looked at me in incredulous horror. "What the hell do you think you are doing?" he shouted. "And who the bloody hell are you anyway?"

With all the dignity I could muster I said, "I am a British officer and I have just arrived from France and Syria."

"You may be the .... King of Siam for all I care!" he snorted. "Come with me while I wake the sergeant!"

In the meantime Ben had joined me and we stood in the middle of the street once again roaring with laughter at the anti-climax of all our hardships. When the sergeant arrived he was equally unimpressed. Seeing two miserable-looking, unkempt civilians in the company of an even more disreputable-looking pair of Arabs he would have returned grumbling to his bed if I had not lost my temper and, putting on my best parade ground manner, told him what I thought of him. This had some effect and taking us with him to the guard house he went to wake his officer.

When the officer finally appeared I took a good look at him and realized to my astonishment that we had been to school together. His name was Peter Kingsett. He remembered my name all right but there his powers of credulity ended. He just could not reconcile the figure he saw in front of him with his far-off school days. However, after this the atmosphere thawed a bit and we were given some strong tea and bully beef with bread. We were certainly back with the British Army!

That night I slept on Peter's li-lo at the foot of his bed while Ben was given some blankets in the guard room. I was amused to see that he could not yet really accept the situation. He slept with his revolver ready to hand!

Next morning we were sent up the line "through the usual channels". First we were driven back to Peter's Battalion Headquarters at Rosh Pinna. Then we were handed on to Brigade at Nazareth where Brigadier Joe Kingston and his staff gave us a wonderful lunch and finally we were processed back to the main Palestine Headquarters in Jerusalem. Although everyone was kindness itself I knew that there was still a lurking suspicion that we might not be who we claimed we were. The suspicion was confirmed when the Brigade Major gave me a letter of introduction to make my reception in Jerusalem easier. It was not sealed so I was able to read it. He wrote: "This is to introduce Captain Lang, who claims to have escaped from France and who came across the frontier early this morning. We think the story is genuine, but consider you should take further steps to check it." My opinion of the British Army's security went up considerably.

It was only when we got to Jerusalem that my identity was at last confirmed beyond any doubt. The Brigade truck delivered us to the Commander-in-Chief's office and I handed my introductory letter to the sentry on the door. The small world proved smaller than ever when two minutes later the General's military secretary appeared. He was none other than my life long friend Harry Cumming Bruce (later Major-General Lord Thurlow) of the Seaforth Highlanders. No prodigal son could have had such a welcome from a parent as I got from Harry. We had last soldiered together in Jerusalem in 1936 and it had not changed much.

I had one more tribulation before I felt I could relax completely and enjoy my freedom. The return to the flesh-pots proved too much for my Marseilles skin bug. Washing my hands in the cloakroom of the luxurious King David

Hotel, I began to itch all over and the symptoms were too familiar to be ignored. I rushed out to a chemist and asked his advice. It was the same as Juliette's—a sulphur bath. I determined that I would have the cure straight away before meeting any more of my friends and accordingly locked myself in one of the hotel bathrooms. Unfortunately I had omitted to take a towel with me. I still blush to think of my return to my own room wrapped in a bath mat and leaving behind me a filthy sulphur-caked bath. I hoped none of the staff connected it with the new British officer who had just arrived.

A few minutes later I took the lift downstairs to join my friends in the bar, smelling slightly of sulphur but otherwise properly dressed in one of Harry's suits.

It was a really wonderful feeling. Even a friendly comment that I needed a haircut, from an old army doctor friend, Ian Young, who had no idea where I had appeared from, did not dent my exhilaration.

177

Epilogue

The first few days of freedom were bliss. I had lived so long in discomfort that I had almost forgotten the little refinements of civilization—having one's shoes cleaned, the morning papers, drinks before luncheon, and so on. To add to my euphoria was the warm feeling that in a few days I would get a posting home for some leave and that I would soon be reunited with my family.

I can still remember the thrill when one of my friends came into the mess in Jerusalem and told me that the Garrison Adjutant wanted to see me, adding, "I think your posting has come through." I absolutely floated round to the office. The Adjutant was the personification of friendliness. "You'll be glad to hear I have some instructions for you at last, Derek," he said. I glowed and waited. "You are to proceed the day after tomorrow to Middle East Headquarters in Cairo."

I nearly fell through the floor. It was not to be home after all but straight back into the war. My rosy picture of the hero's return died a sudden death. The Adjutant misunderstood my woebegone expression. "Cheer up", he said, "I don't think they will give you a staff job. You will be with your regiment in the desert in no time."

His forecast was accurate. I spent a short time sharing a flat in Cairo's Garden City and had the great privilege of an hour with General Wavell, who asked me many questions about German behaviour as I had experienced it and about the attitude of the French. Then, early in December, I paid a social visit to the 2nd Camerons in the Western Desert.

It was when I was there that I learned with some alarm, because I had had no experience of desert warfare, that I was expected to take over command of a Company. This proved unfounded but shortly afterwards, in January, the 2nd Camerons were sent to the Sudan, ready to strike into Eritrea and I joined them as Adjutant at Kassala, last visited in 1935.

In June we were back in the desert and took part in the march from Mersa Matruh to Sidi Barrani, the prelude to the disastrous operation "Battle Axe" which involved an attack on Libya from Egypt via the Halfaya Pass. It was during this operation that I was very nearly captured again. The regiment was practically encircled and I found myself giving my friends advice on what to pack in their haversacks to make escape easier. In fact we managed to get out of the net but it was a close shave. It was almost a year to the day after my first capture.

There followed some staff training at Haifa and then a period on the staff of S.O.E. in Cairo, sending agents to Yugoslavia, Greece and Crete. It was while in Haifa that I was able to return to Syria, which had by then been liberated by the Free French and ourselves, and thank the many who had helped Ben and me cross the frontier. That poor Arab driver who had taken us into the hills thought he was seeing a ghost when we met again, now that I was properly turned out as an Army Major. Ben had written to me that he had arrived in Britain and was with de Gaulle's forces at home.

At the end of 1942, I sailed for England, via South Africa, to take up an appointment at the School of Infantry. I was still there on "D" Day, but shortly afterwards I received a signal to proceed to France to take command of a Battalion of the Cameronians. This was a great disappointment to me for, without any reflection on the Cameronians, I was, naturally, most anxious to rejoin the new Highland Division and, particularly, my own regiment. I discussed the matter with my boss, Brigadier Harry Houldsworth, who had been wounded with us in 1940, and it was agreed that a message should be sent back saying "Not available", which was the equivalent of saying that I did not want a command job. By return there came the rather petulant reply, "Cannot understand Lang not available to command 5th Camerons which he helped to form." So much for signal errors!

My joy knew no bounds and within twenty-four hours I was across the Channel. I took over the 5th Camerons while they were still in the invasion bridgehead. Shortly afterwards we broke out from Caen and started the victorious march of liberation through France. As we approached St Valéry the whole of the Highland Division were keyed up. There were few amongst us who had been there in the fateful days of 1940 but everyone seemed to have a sense of the greatness of the occasion. I am sure that none, however, could have looked forward to taking part in the recapture more than I did.

The Highland Division was commanded by Major-General Tom Rennie who had been on General Victor Fortune's staff in 1940 and had escaped, and he now showed why he earned such affection from those who served under him. Jack Walford and Bill Bradford commanding the 5th Seaforth and 5th Black Watch, respectively, had also been with the Division in 1940. Tom Rennie arranged with Jim Cassels, our Brigadier (now a Field-Marshal), that Jack and I should lead our Battalions into the town, one from the east, the other from the west, ahead of the rest of the

Division. We were deeply grateful to our General and Brigadier. It was 2 September.

The Germans had evacuated St Valéry two days before our arrival so there was no one to interfere with our day of triumph. As my leading Company, preceded by five pipers, marched into the town's main square, the local population went wild with delight. Then there were speeches and drinks all round as formality gave way to a free-for-all. I can remember in particular one young lady who appeared wearing an authentic Cameron kilt which she had kept safely hidden for four years. For a moment I feared that, in the enthusiasm of the moment, she was going after all to lose it. In the end, however, her modesty was preserved and I got a photograph of her with two of my pipers.

That night I went to bed a very excited but a very happy man. Regiments were deployed around St Valéry as they had been before the surrender.

The reaction to our triumphal entry into the town came the next day when I made a pilgrimage round the British cemeteries looking for the graves of my comrades. I am happy to say that they had all been beautifully kept, but there were few of the names I sought. All too often the inscriptions on the crosses simply read "*Soldat Anglais, inconnu*".

On a more light-hearted note I also set out to see if I could find my tin trunk which had been so carefully buried. As Murdo Shand, my batman, who had buried it, was languishing as a P.O.W. I was on a wild goose chase. However, later that day the man who had helped Murdo bury it reported the matter to the authorities and it was recovered. It was, alas, not worth the trouble. The box was there but the ants had done their worst and all that I got back was a ragged patch from my tartan breeches and some buttons which I kept as souvenirs.

I would dearly have liked to have walked the four miles along the beach to Veules-les-Roses as I had done before but time did not permit. Anyway, the whole coastline had changed with the massive defences which the Germans had built everywhere. There were pill-boxes built into the cliffs, houses transformed into camouflaged gun emplacements and masses of barbed wire. Only one thing remained unchanged. On the beach at Veules-les-Roses the little British tanker still lay in the sand where we had left her four years earlier.

We stayed in St Valéry for two days and during that time I was billeted with the Mayor of a small hamlet about two miles out of the town. To my astonishment I found myself sharing the Mayor's hospitality with three old ladies who had been evacuated from the town, and one of them I immediately recognized. She, with her two sisters, were the owners of the Villa Elizabett where I had arrived soaking wet with shells dropping all around, seeking a place to sleep on that last dreadful night in 1940. I will never forget the imperturbable way in which she invited me in and offered to dry my clothes as if I were just paying a social call.

In the course of conversation with these three heroines, one of them asked me if I knew Roddy Mackay "Most certainly," I said, in great surprise, "he was my unit doctor!" This occasioned great excitement and she rushed off and returned with a fine sheep-skin jacket which Roddy had left with her for safe-keeping and which she had guarded zealously ever since.

The nostalgia occasioned by my return to St Valéry was only the start for me of a sentimental journey which I had promised myself.

From St Valéry I went to Forges-les-Faux, where it was strange to see British troops billeted in comfort where we had been in such squalor. The old caretaker and his wife who had sold us additions to our rations were still there.

The citadel at Doullens was empty except for a few French troops and I was able to wander as I wished through the deserted rooms which had once been our prison; then I drove to St Pol where I had had to deliver the speech to hundreds of mutinous soldiers; then I went in search of the hole in the hedge through which we had dived on our first escape. I found it but the hedge itself had been cut low and would have been quite incapable of concealing us as it had four years ago. I looked high and low for the "Pouillys", the first people who had helped us, but, sadly, never traced them.

After that I went to Le Touquet and then on to St Cecile where the fat German on his horse had taken us prisoner for the second time. Our bathing hut had gone, now transformed into a deep concrete shelter, but the cafe still remained on the opposite side of the road and to my delight I recognized the proprietress behind the counter. Poor dear! When I made myself known to her she burst into tears. She remembered us well and was so upset that she had failed us by only letting us buy sweets. I told her that there was little else she could have done with the Germans billeted literally next door but it was a long time before she would be comforted.

At Camiers it was a different story. I went immediately to the cafe where they had been so kind to us but it was owned by strangers. After a few enquiries, however, I discovered our good samaritan living in a house nearby. When she opened the door she recognized me instantly. How she identified me with the bearded, bedraggled creature who had come to her for help in 1940, I don't know, but her joy at seeing me again was most touching. She was obviously penniless, but she insisted on my having a cup of coffee and pressed on me a glass of her meagre supply of cognac. For me it was a most moving encounter.

And so my journey of memories continued—to the barracks at Montreuil where we had watched the Germans from our prison window doing their training, to the Caserne Kléber where I was able to thank the school mistress in person for her bag of sugar and on to the barracks at Tournai from which Johnnie and I had finally made our escape. I climbed on to the roof of the outhouse with great difficulty and looked down again over the wall. The drop seemed more formidable than ever and it was amazing to me that we had both managed it without mishap.

All the time my journey was bringing me nearer to the moment when I would be able to meet again all the people who had helped us so much in and around Lille. Now I sought out Sally's house with a great sense of foreboding. There had been rumours that she had been finally caught by the Germans and that she was in a concentration camp. Because I had seen so little of the house from the outside, I feared that I would have difficulty locating it, but when I entered the street my doubts were resolved by seeing an enormous Union Jack outside one house, flying side by side with the Tricolour of France and the Stars and Stripes. Imagine my frantic joy when I rang the bell to have it answered by Sally herself with Siegfried, the great Dane, by her side. She was fit and well and as trim as ever in her Red Cross uniform. Our delight at seeing each other again at first made communication between us almost impossible. We both had so many questions to ask that we could hardly wait to hear the answers. Once inside the house I rushed around it as if it was my own. It was almost unchanged. Still the same old radio and the rack of pipes which I had tried one after the other. There was the yard where I had tramped night after night for exercise and the piano still stood where it had always done.

Now my enemy was time. I was due soon to return to my unit and there were so many people I wanted to see and so much to learn. As we talked Sally's young nephew, Jean, arrived in his uniform of a sous-officier in the Free French Army—a very sophisticated version of the young boy who had brought us food and books to the little flat down the street. Then there was a hurried visit to "Mama". Two of the girls were also at home and they rushed me up to see the attic where we had all lived so tightly packed. Mama was as gay as ever, looking a little older perhaps but none the worse for her experiences. Her old husband had sadly died a year before.

In between times I was able to gather a little of Sally's own experiences under the Nazis. She had been taken in a dozen times for questioning under third degree conditions and she had been twice arrested, but, miraculously, she had escaped being sent to a concentration camp. In spite of the fact that the Germans were keeping a close eye on her, she carried on her work during the whole of the occupation. When the supply of B.E.F. escapees had dried up she had become involved in helping British and American airmen who had been shot down. If any woman deserved a British decoration for her bravery it was Sally but, although I tried very hard on her behalf, she never got one.

Of Georges she had heard nothing since he had left, but she believed he had finally got to Algeria. Oddly enough, she received a telegram from him a week after I left saying that he was on his way home. I was later to hear his full story which I will soon recount.

There was just time before I left the Lille area to drive out to Pont Thibault. We raced out past the airfield, now manned by the R.A.F. and pulled in first at Alice's farm.

It was a shock when the door was opened by a complete stranger who had not the slightest idea what I was talking about. Somewhat chastened we next called on Monsieur Vaubeck, the wine merchant, and to my relief found him and his wife in great heart. I had to eat a large feast washed down with copious quantities of drink before I was allowed to make my next call.

Much as I enjoyed seeing them again and appreciated their overwhelming hospitality, I could hardly wait to get to the Mailles farm where I had spent so long and enjoyed such kindness. I was near to tears when I greeted them again and I think they were equally moved. In no time at all the word went round that "*Pierre*" was back and soon the house was filled with well-wishers. Among the first was Lucille, who had tried so hard to teach me French, followed by the pork butcher, who was quite insulted when I tried to repay him the hundred francs he had lent me.

Alice, I learned, had died the previous year and my old friend, François, at Stork Farm, was also dead. The Depuis were still going strong and asked anxiously after the two Yorkshire boys, Arthur and Daniel. I was only able to tell them that they had been recaptured and were safe in a prison camp in Germany. Monsieur Depuis had had his own adventures, having been put in prison twice by the Germans for contravening the game laws. After Georges I have never known anyone who disliked the Germans more.

The time sped by and long before we had exhausted our gossip, I had to leave. I drove back to rejoin my battalion full of wonder at the incredible luck Johnnie and I had had in meeting such marvellous people in our wanderings. Without their courage and devotion our chances of avoiding a prisoner of war cage would have been remote indeed.

It was some time after this first sentimental journey that

I was able to catch up with some of the other friends who had helped us on our way, but among the first I was able to visit was Kitty in Paris who, with Sally, and Madame Maille, were the people most instrumental in my escape.

Kitty's story was a horrifying one. Shortly after she had seen us on our way to Bordeaux she was arrested and imprisoned in Paris where she was subjected to the most dreadful tortures in an effort to get her to reveal the names of her accomplices. They had removed her fingernails one by one and reduced her to a complete physical wreck before they gave up and sent her to a concentration camp in Germany. She survived even this, but the signing of the Armistice was not the end of her ordeal. She was then in the Russian Zone and with other inmates of the camp was forced into a brothel for Russian soldiers. It was six months after peace had been signed before she managed to make her way back to Paris. By this time she weighed only five stone.

I am happy to say that in Kitty's case her extraordinary bravery was recognized by both Britain and France, by whom she was awarded the MBE and the Croix de Guerre, respectively. Both Colin Hunter and I saw much of Kitty in the fifteen years after the war, either in France or Britain before she died. She stayed with me twice in Scotland, bringing her two grandsons with her. Colin and I were two of the few mourners at her funeral in London. Although always a Paris resident she died in her country of birth in the London Hospital.

It was 1951 before I was able to get back to Marseilles. Of course in the meantime I had kept in touch by letter and had been well supplied with photographs of my old friends and their growing families. Just the same it was a great thrill for me to shake Lulu by the hand again and have a meal in the familiar old cafe. He was now the proud godfather of one of Odette's children and still the same generous, big-hearted buccaneer. My beloved Juliette, at whose hands I had suffered so severely with her sulphur treatments was now happily married, as I was myself, but we were overjoyed to see each other again and laugh about the old days.

I was glad to learn that most of my friends had managed to make good their escape from Marseilles. I already knew that Johnnie had managed to escape through Spain in the spring of 1941 and had been returned home from Gibraltar. He nearly died from typhus in a Spanish hospital. Colin, with a number of others, managed to persuade the medical authorities that their wounds warranted repatriation and were duly despatched to Britain.

I was to hear the full story of Georges' exploits. Unable to fulfil his ambition of joining General de Gaulle in London, he managed to get across to Algiers where he quickly made a name for himself as a skilful surgeon and as an outspoken critic of Marshal Pétain. He was in the thick of the fight when the Allies arrived in Algeria and later took an active part in the Italian campaign. All his three sons went into the army. His eldest son was a parachutist before his early death and his youngest was later killed at Dien Bien Phu. Georges himself was mentioned in despatches and awarded the Cross of Liberation and the Legion of Honour. He was also awarded a second Croix de Guerre, having won his first one in the 1914–18 war.

When we parted company in Marseilles I was determined that we would meet again so that I could thank him properly for all his help. We were to meet but he could not receive my gratitude properly. I traced him to a house in Lille in 1960 where he was slowly dying, tended by his sister. Sally and he had separated after the war. He died two years later and his sister sent me a copy of the address

point it can be said that the full circle wa[s]
David Murray was commanding and A[n]
Adjutant and they accompanied me on
of that English General almost a quarte[r]
whose travels had not been so smooth [as]

It was a fascinating experience for [me]
the part of the tour which took me to th[e]
There in the Post Office at Lochbois[d]
lennan, once one of our trusted Sergea[nts]
job as postmaster—a few more grey hair[s]
in my memory.

That great character, Finlay Macke[nzie]
longer present. He had died some yea[rs]
I had visited him when he was bedri[dden]
remember how, despite doctor's and h[is nurs]-
ing wife's orders, he had insisted on [being]
with me as we reminisced.

Returning from some loch fishing [I was]
driving with Angus along a particular[ly lonely]
road in South Uist when we observed [an]
old man approaching. It was obvious
that something stronger than water ha[d]
he wa[s] steering a course which was far [from straight]
we drew alongside, however, he co[lle]c[t]
[e]ently and drawing up with pride t[o]
us to a well-executed salute.

"One of your territorials," I said,
"No, General," replied Angus p[roudly]
one of yours!"

By 1966 I was Army Commande[r]
Caskie was again in evidence as one [of]
was installed as Governor of Edinbu[rgh]
the summer of 1969 that the twenty-fif[th]
liberation of St Valéry was celebrated.

given at his grave. She also told me that he had recognized me when I had called and that my visit had greatly comforted him. Sally moved from Lille to near Lyons and I once visited her there. We corresponded regularly but now all is silent, so I fear she must have died too.

Of the three main French "foster mothers" only Madame Maille is alive. I took my son, Simon, to stay with her and her husband, François, in Ennevelin and I was given my old room, which was most nostalgic. In 1971, my wife and I spent the evening with the Maille family—and what an evening it was—whilst motoring home from the Pyrénées. We sat down twelve of a family round that table so familiar to me and the fatted calf was well and truly killed. François senior was no more but François junior, married with children, runs the farm. Michel, the younger brother, also married, is a prosperous merchant in Lille. Petit Pierre was also present. To crown everything Madame Maille with one of her sisters visited Scotland on a 'bus tour two months later despite her seventy-five years and came to stay with us in Perthshire. Much to her embarrassment she received much publicity when I was Chieftain for the Crieff Annual Games.

There remain only a few loose ends to tie up before my story is complete.

In 1962, my military career having prospered far beyond anything I could have expected in the dark days of 1940, I found myself in command of the 51st Division and as such, in partnership with the Division's great commander in North Africa, Douglas Wimberley, closely concerned with the organization of the first great reunion of its past and present members which took place a year later. For we older soldiers in particular it was a tremendous occasion.

When the great day arrived there were twenty thousand of us assembled on the North Inch in Perth. There was

every type of contest, athletic and ⬚
bands of all the Highland Regime⬚
freshment tents—one for each Re⬚
in a great flood. It was a day of go⬚
fellowship and reminiscence. The ⬚
legion but perhaps the meeting I re⬚
when I came face to face with the ⬚
who had befriended Johnnie and ⬚
were many men in that great ga⬚
to be grateful to him, and not the ⬚

There is also a sadness about ⬚
inescapable. One cannot help thi⬚
companions who would have rejo⬚
us but had not lived to see the ⬚
generally mourned was the late M⬚
Fortune who had commanded us a⬚
said to be the British General mo⬚
mans in the last war. He was cer⬚
and there was a lump in many ⬚
widow, Lady Fortune, stood up ⬚
special cheer came forth when she⬚
to her son, who was then comma⬚
Black Watch.

Jock Crichton, my Assistant in ⬚
the Highland Division. He organize⬚
last reunion in 1967 on Perth's ⬚
Marshal Montgomery as the guest ⬚
that the Division, which soon after ⬚
in a blaze of glory.

It was in 1964 that I was able ⬚
dearest ambitions. It is the custom ⬚
mander to choose annually one of ⬚
command for inspection in detail. ⬚
now renamed the 4/5th Camerons ⬚

on the heights above the town in an army aeroplane and was greeted with the greatest ceremony by all the assembled dignitaries. Behind all the formality and the speeches, however, there was still the same warmth that there had always been.

Two months later I took the salute at my last tattoo at Edinburgh Castle with the Mayor of St Valéry-en-Caux by my side as my guest of honour. We shared the luxury of the box seats with fifty of my old comrades of the 4th and 5th Camerons.

Within a few days my career in the Army was finally over. For me it could not have ended on a more fitting note.

(See inset, right)

PARIS

BORDEAUX • • LIBOURNE

LA RÉOLE •

TOULOUSE •

MARSEILLES •

KEY

- - - ▶ - - - Route of 2ⁿᵈ escape